CHEIRO'S MEMOIRS

CHEIRO'S MEMOIRS

THE REMINISCENCES OF A SOCIETY PALMIST

INCLUDING INTERVIEWS WITH
KING EDWARD THE SEVENTH
W. E. GLADSTONE, C. S. PARNELL, H. M. STANLEY, MADAME
SARAH BERNHARDT, OSCAR WILDE, PROFESSOR MAX MULLER,
BLANCI-tE ROOSEVELT, THE COMTE DE PARIS, JOSEPH CHAM-
BERLAIN, LORD RUSSELL OF KILLOWEN, ROBERT INGERSOLL,
ELLA WHEELER WILCOX, MRS. LANGTRY, "MARK TWAIN," W.
T. STEAD, RICHARD CROKER, MLLE. JANOTHA, AND OTHERS

WITH TWENTY-ONE ILLUSTRATIONS

ISBN: 978-1-957990-03-3

Contents

"Cheiro"

PREFACE

Memories, like jewels, are sometimes bright, some times clouded, but, alas! by those who attempt to make their setting too elaborate. If I have erred by endeavouring to set these Memories in too simple a style it is not because I have not appreciated seriously enough the privilege of meeting such great personalities as King Edward VII., W. E. Gladstone, H. M. Stanley, Joseph Chamberlain, Lord Russell of Killowen, Charles Stewart Parnell, Mark Twain, and others, but, on the contrary, because I have felt that such names, being already set in the Temple of Time, required no elaborate phrases of mine to add to their glory.

"Cheiro."

FOREWORD

I BELIEVE I am justified in saying that no other person in modern times raised a branch of one of the so-called occult studies to a greater perfection or position of respect than I did during the period in which I was known professionally as " Cheiro."

I make this statement in all humbleness, well realising that the particular talent for such work was " given " me for some purpose-as such I treated the" gift," and endeavoured to return it as one would a loan-if possible increased in value. No one deplores more than I do that my success has been followed by many imitators who have little aptitude or knowledge for occult studies of any kind, and so have since brought discredit on such pursuits. Some have gone so far as even to copy the name I took for my nom de guerre, but this alone is sufficient to prove that,as they have not had enough brains to make a name for themselves, they cannot have the requisite mental power to proceed far in occult studies.

Excellence in any branch of occultism is attained by the same effort it is necessary to make in order to succeed in any other art, science, or profession. To paint pictures, the artist must first have the necessary temperament, the patience to study for years, and the courage to withstand the thousand and one disappointments that assail him on every side.

In science it is the same. Yet think what study with the proper temperament can produce! To the botanist the simplest leaf may tell the story of the tree, or to the zoologist the smallest fragment of a bone may tell the history of a race.

Apply the same rules to the student of human nature and you must concede that every line may also have its language and may tell the very thought or motive which produced it or called it into being.

The soul in its prison-house is continually trying to send out messages through the bars of custom, conventionality, and hypocrisy.

Such messages may only be read by those who have "ears to hear" and "eyes to see," but it does not make them any the less real because the great crowd of humanity have heard nothing but their own cries or seen nothing but their own afflictions.

Science has proved that even metals have their occult or unknown qualities-stones attract stones and atoms are drawn towards atoms by an intangible "something" called affinity.

What then of the " affinities" of human beings, not only to one another, but to inanimate things, such as names, places, and numbers ?

Inanimate is, however, the wrong word, for there is nothing without life, and so a Number may be as much a living force for good or evil as the greatest man or woman who exists.

As " even a sparrow cannot fall   to the ground" without its Creator being conscious, so the smallest action bears its part equal to that of the greatest in the heart-throb of the Infinite. Has it ever occurred to you that as there is a moment fixed for life to begin and another moment for it to end, between the two points the years, the days, the hours, and even the minutes may also fit into their appointed actions?

A great philosopher has said that the universe is built on mathematics and that "God geometrises down to the smallest fraction of time/' If this is so, why should you so dislike to think that your little life should obey the same laws, or that the soul within responds to the pulse of God, as do all other things in life?

Believe such thoughts or not, as you will, we, the students of the occult or the soul life of things, may do our duty as nobly as others in our seeking for the reason of what we see. We may also work through days of toil and sleepless nights, or spend long years with faith alone to feed the lamp of hope, but in the end, if our discoveries should enable us to translate another word in the message of life, surely not even the veriest sceptic would say that such students have worked in vain.

"CHEIRO."
DEVONSHIRE LODGE
IS MARYLEBONE ROAD LONDON, W.

CHAPTER I

THE MAKING OF A SEER : THE " CALL OF LONDON" : CHARLES STEWART PARNELL

FROM many sides I have been requested to publish my memoirs, but there are certain reasons which have kept me for years from doing so, the most important being that it is so difficult to write about one's self, so hard to take the sheaf of memory apart, to know where to begin and where to leave off.

For a long time I have endeavoured to avoid the publication of this book, and I might continue to do so for a still longer period if my own desire could be the deciding factor ; but in this strange world of facts, fancies, and fallacies one is sometimes obliged to put forward the facts, lest the fallacies of others get too strong a headway.

It is so with me. If I did not publish this book, others would have done so for me ; and in that case I fear fiction might have become stranger than truth.

My only claim to "notoriety" is, that in pursuing an unusual career I naturally had unusual experiences, and in many instances met unusual people.

It is these people and experiences that have a claim on the interest of the general public-my own life must only be regarded as the thread on which Destiny hung her pearls or her puppets, as the case may be.

I will therefore relate as little of my own personal life as possible, and if the white thread of self should at times come to the surface, I trust it may only be considered as the connecting link that it was impossible to eliminate altogether.

As the frailest thread must have a beginning,

I will therefore in as few words as possible touch on my early life, but only that part of it which bears on the curious study which I subsequently made so peculiarly my own.

Briefly, then, the thread started as follows: On my father's side I am of Norman descent, on my mother's from a French family, born in Ireland, and I may say almost bred on books.

From my father's side I inherited poetry, pride, and philosophy, from my mother's, love of the occult in every form, combined with a curious religious devotionalism which has never ceased to exist.

The subsequent fusion in the fires of life of this peculiar combination naturally produced a being predestined for a career that would not run on conventional lines.

As the simplest things become the turning points in men as in worlds, so an unusually wet Sunday was the main factor in changing the current of my destiny. Briefly, to prevent my disturbing my father writing poems in the library, my mother-who understood well the study of hands-taught me the names of the lines in my own and sent me off to find, if it were possible, a hand with similar markings.

I was only a little past eleven then, yet that seed of thought instantly took root; so much so, that when I had exhausted the servants' hands I essayed the village, a mile away, and it was only the next day, after a long and weary search, that my grief-stricken parents discovered my whereabouts, and the youthful scientist was dragged home and put to bed.

Shortly afterwards, perhaps to combat my occult tendencies, my father decided that I should be trained for the Church, and I was accordingly sent to an extremely strict school, where my father was assured that all such non sense as occultism would be quickly knocked out of my head.

In his idea of training me for the Church he was, I believe, right; for I am certain no boy ever began life with a more religious nature or a more devotional temperament.

Although, at first sight, it may perhaps seem a strange anomaly, yet I hold that it was the essentials of that very temperament that made me cling to the study of hands with an obstinacy that surmounted all opposition.

It was a mystery like religion itself, it contained the language of the soul £nits prison house, and the lines in the hand seemed many a time to me a more tangible chart of life than the Thirty-nine Articles that I was forced to commit to memory.

It was also despised of men, a much abused, slandered, calumniated something, that attracted me out of very sympathy and compassion. Thus it was that the more I studied Scripture, the more the strange threads of destiny seemed to bind life, actions and results together; and the more I became convinced that Nature had her secret pages that neither Science nor Religion had as yet unravelled.

I cannot describe with what joy I discovered text after text in that great "Book of Fate" that told of the destinies of races, and those strange happenings "that the will of God might be fulfilled."

Can I ever forget that night when my mind grasped for the first time the story of the Betrayed and the betrayer; the picture of the "Man of Sorrows" and that Child of Destiny called Judas-the one necessary to the other " that the Scriptures might be fulfilled " ?

As I sat there in the silence, trying to balance the "whys" and the "wherefores," it seemed as if the fate-stricken face of Judas formed from the • shadows _ of the past, and in his weak, out stretched hands I read the heredity that fitted him for his role, and that left his name the by word of the nations-as they also fill their destiny, write their record, and are gone.

The next day the Scriptures had a greater meaning for me than ever, the Thirty-nine Articles possessed a fascination that amazed the reverend professor of my class, and the seventeenth, with its magnificent argument for "predestination," became such a force in my thoughts that before I could realise what I was doing I gave battle on the subject to my astonished teacher, and got punished by the losing of the play hour for my pains.

But as out of every evil comes good-that is, if we will only try to distinguish the good when it does come-so during my punishment, instead of doing my exercises, I sketched what I thought ought to have been the hands of Judas, and be came so absorbed in my task that I did not feel the presence of the old professor looking over my shoulder.

Instead of the sharp reproof I expected, the old man on the contrary sat down by my side and made me explain the drawing to him, line by line. Then he became still more friendly, and then-to my utter blank astonishment-he held out his own long, curious-looking hands, and in quite a gentle way asked me what I could make out of them.

To my amazement I quickly discovered traits that were even human. To me he had ever been something so high and mighty that the idea of this monument of wisdom having lived as other men had never for a moment entered my mind.

He was a long, lean, gaunt, anatomical structure, on which I thought some one had hung a clergyman's coat in order to hide the bones; a hollow-jawed, grey-eyed, spectacled Sphinx, that history said had once stroked the Cambridge eight to victory-but history tells so many lies that none of us boys believed the story; yet, as I warmed up to my study, I forgot that history also said that he had never known emotion of any kind-that he had never loved-had never married ; yet I was telling him of a love in his life that few men have met with, and have cared to live life out afterwards.

I stopped, for something had gone wrong with my subject ; the hands had been pulled aside and I beheld, for the first time, what tears mean when stern men weep.

After that morning we became friends. Many a difficult exercise he let me off, and many an old Greek and Latin book on hands he translated for my benefit.

The Church was, however, not my destiny. On the very eve of my entering her service my father was ruined by a speculation that involved hundreds of others; and so, almost broken hearted at the fading away of my hopes, I returned home.

Disappointed and purposeless, I drifted for some time like a helmless ship on an idle sea, until at last one day some undercurrent from where I know not woke me again, and I entered my father's study and told him I wanted to steer my own bark, and see the world for myself.

My father considered he had no longer the right to mould my career to his will-he had tried, but destiny had been too strong-he would let destiny have her way. So, with a small amount of money and a good, substantial blessing, I spread my own sails and leaving the quiet harbour of home I drifted out into the world's wide sea like so many others have done before me.

It would be out of place in these memoirs to enter into some few intervening experiences; the " Call of London " was in my ears, and so as quickly as possible I forsook the temptation of quieter routes and steered direct to that Great City where Fate meets Ambition in equal combat. It is said that "coming events cast their shadows before them." One night, while waiting in Liverpool for the London train, my eyes caught sight of a book with a hand drawn on the cover, which I immediately bought. It was a translation of one of those books on palmistry that had been printed at the same time that the Bible was first printed with movable type ; it was called in German "Die Kunst Ciromanta," and as the train started on its journey I became at once engrossed in its contents.

The only other occupant of the carriage was a gentleman who sat opposite with his back to the engine, and had wrapped round his shoulders a heavy rug that almost concealed his face. When, however, my book was finished, as I laid it down I noticed that his sharp eyes were fixed intently on the drawing of the hand that adorned the cover. As I put it aside, in a genial but rather bantering way he said: " So you evidently believe in hand-reading. An odd kind of study it must be. But I suppose," he added, "it can find its followers, as people believe in the shape of the head, and other things of the kind."

"Yes," I answered, "I believe that character makes itself manifest in every portion of the body, but naturally more especially in the hands, which are, after all, the tools that carry out the wishes of the brain; and surely there is nothing so far-fetched or illogical in such a belief."

"No," he said laughingly. "Compared with some beliefs, that sounds both moderate and reasonable. But do the hands tell the future? That is the point that would appeal to me, if I could bring myself to believe in such a thing."

"Well," I replied, "as far as our future is made and influenced by our character and the tendencies we have inherited, I certainly believe they do, and as success is really the result of the preponderance of our strong points over our weaknesses, I think one might be safe in saying that, looking at the study from this standpoint alone, the hands may be able to show which of these two forces will gain the mastery."

"Good," he answered. "Your theory has really interested me." And, stretching out his hands, he said: "Tell me, if you will, which will gain .the victory in my case."

I can even now see those slender, intellectual• looking hands that this stranger laid before me, and how they interested me, line after line clearly marked, full of character, and of events created by character. I started by the Line of Mentality. I showed him its superior length to those of some of the designs in my book, and explained to him that it denoted his power of will, of organisation and of command over people. Then I called his attention to a well-marked Line of Destiny that was strongly traced through his hand until a little past the centre of the palm, and I explained that it indicated strong individuality, a career that must play a marked role in life-a destiny, in fact, that would cause him to stand out as a leader above the common herd of humanity.

"But the end," he said almost nervously. "What does that line show by fading out-what does it mean? "

I laughed as I said it, for I could hardly believe, and I felt sure he would not, in spite of his interest. " Oh," I said, "the stopping of that sign simply means rest for you; another Napoleon sent to St. Helena, I suppose."

"But why?" he said rather excitedly. "What shall be my Waterloo?"

"A woman, without a doubt," I replied. "You see yourself how the Line of Heart breaks the Line of Destiny just below that point where it fades out." Taking his hand away, the stranger laughed-a low, quiet laugh-the laugh of a man who was sure of himself.

Shortly afterwards the train rushed into Euston, and as we got our valises and sticks ready he said:

"It's strange, but that science of yours has been curiously accurate about some things except about the woman part. There is my card; you will see now how in some things it tallies but the woman, no-a man with my life has no time for women." And with a cheery" Goodbye" he jumped out, hailed a hansom, and was off.

Looking down at the card, I read, " Charles Stewart Parnell."

It was some years later, after the O'Shea divorce case and his downfall, that I got over my surprise and was able to understand the meaning of the Heart Line touching the destiny of such a man.

CHAPTER II

As this is a resume of a special career, I will not enter into any details of my personal experiences in London, but will only deal with the events that led up to the career in question. Suffice it to say that after a short while the desire for travel became so strong that at last, without much thought as to why or whither I went, I took passage on a trading vessel bound for India, and after a more or less uneventful voyage I reached Bombay.

While there I came in contact with a certain sect of Brahmins, descendants of those who, thousands of years before the Christian era, had evolved by study a science called Samudrika, or the meaning .of the expression of the lines of the . body, and who later evolved from that again a higher study called Hastirika, or the science of the science of Samudrika, or, in other words, the Science of the Lines of the Hand.

After in this way completing my education in the land of the birth of the study that had for such a long time fascinated me, I returned to London, and as during my absence I had in herited a considerable amount of money through the death of a relation, I was consequently free to carry out my fancy, and for some time (like a man who had a hobby for collecting stamps or old coins)-1 visited hospitals, and even prisons, to collect impressions of hands of all sorts and conditions of humanity.

But the love of travel and of Oriental countries, and the distaste for ordinary civilisation which I had acquired during the simple life I had led in India, turned my wanderings towards another land of mystery, namely, Egypt; and so for a certain time I occupied myself with ruined tombs, temples, and kindred things in that land where the children of occultism had built their pyramids. On my return to Cairo I received the news that the man whom I had left to take care of my interests in London had embezzled everything I possessed, and I was left without a penny.

It was at this moment that my study of hands was for the first time called into practical purpose; and in my rooms in Cairo I made sufficient money by it to enable me to return to London to see after my affairs.

Affairs, however, there were none, for all assets had gone ; and the unfortunate man who had brought about such a result had disappeared from life's arena by the door of suicide.

Such being the case, I set about facing life from a new standpoint. I developed a literary tendency, which I had scarcely dreamt I possessed. At all events, it enabled me to live, and even to enjoy life in a very simple way.

Those who have never lived the "simple life" will not, perhaps, realise the pleasures that one can find in a top room of a seven-story house looking over the Embankment-the subdued dull roar of the great city at one's feet; the sob and sigh of the river of life as its tides ebb at night, and flow again with the coming of the day. In the distance one may see the Thames with its gliding craft and its long stretch of silver and blue and green, as it gleams under the skies of June or becomes grey and grim with a November night, or hides itself in the folds of some yellow fog-yellow as the wrappings of the mummies that hold the past of Egypt in their deathless sleep.

In a room on the top of a seven-story house one's anxieties are also less-one never sees one's enemies, and one's friends may be few, but they must be real if they ever reach one's door.

From such a point of vantage one does not see the horrors of life, the daily brutality of the streets, the starving faces that rise in the crowd and disappear again, like the bubbles that float on some muddy stream-all these things one does not see, and so a seventh-floor abode has often considerable advantages.

Linked up with my new calling, again there cropped up the study of hands. A mysterious murder was committed in the East End, and a blood-stained hand mark on the paint of a door called my study into question. An examination of the lines of the hands of the murdered man told me, from similar marks in the blood stained impression, that the crime was undoubtedly done by a relation, and this clue led to the arrest and subsequent confession of one of the dead man's relatives, who up to then had been the least suspected.

But at this period nothing was farther from my wishes than to practise such a study from a professional standpoint. I was not perhaps yet ready for the work, and so I continued as before, but with the exception that I devoted all my spare time to studying hands wherever I could get the opportunity; and so adding to the collection which I had always stored up from my earliest days.

Evidently I was not yet ready to preach the truth of what I believed in (how easily one can see the steps of fate as one looks backward !) ; I bad no self-confidence, the sensitiveness was too sharp, it had to be ground down yet by the mills of life-those mills of experience that crush some to death and grind others to fit the groove in fortune's wheel that may one day carry them onward to success.

However, the gift of writing, or call it what ever you like, soon faded or changed, or for the time being died out; it had played its part, a step perhaps towards the next; but whatever it was, the faculty that wrote no longer suited the buyers-it may have been that it did better work

I   am not the judge-those who pay have evidently got the right in such matters ; but the fact remains that the manuscripts came back by every post-and the poems that some religious papers had always accepted before, were returned with regrets, and sometimes a pencilled line to say, "Style changed, not suitable for our pages." A grey October morning found me returning from Fleet Street towards the Strand, utterly dispirited after an interview with an editor of a certain religious paper, a man who had taken sufficient interest in something I had written to ask me to call had found the Rev. Dr. -- the most humane editor I had ever met. To my profound astonishment he had pulled up an arm-chair close to mine, and in the kindest manner he had talked to me as a father would to his son. He pointed out the changes that had taken place in my verses and articles in the past few months, and where in place of the devotional tone in which I had at first written, there now appeared ideas and expressions that he said could not possibly be penned by the same person.

This splendid old man, who could so easily recognise evolution in races or in worlds, could not realise the same evolution in the brain ; to him I was a young man deliberately choosing " the broad road," and his duty was done when he had told me so, and yet it was almost with tears in his eyes that he added that I was between "the two roadways," in other words: on that narrow strip of thorny ground between the " broad path" that leads to-he graphically implied where, by a significant motion of his hand-and that other path that is evidently so narrow that it accommodates but very few people.

In my own mind, as I returned back up Fleet Street, I translated his words to be exactly what I felt, namely, that I was in "the ditch " and had scarcely even the strength left to scramble out.

But life is ever so-the changes in its pathway are often only hidden by the breaks that we think we cannot get over. In a few minutes I was about to scramble out of "my ditch," but on which side I got I will leave my readers to decide in accordance with their own views, for I have long since learned that as the different chords in music make their own harmony-so the different opinions of people also vibrate in accordance with the position in which they have themselves been placed in the harp of Life.

We only make discords when we attempt to force our views of right or wrong upon our fellows.

Better then let each one strike his own chord-leaving to the great Musician of the Universe the finding of the melody.

CHAPTER III

I HAD just got beyond Somerset House on my weary tramp towards my seventh-floor abode, when I met a man of decidedly Jewish appearance who looked sharply at me as I passed.

As I had somehow always associated Jews with money, I wondered why this man looked at me so curiously, and I walked on, turning his look over and over in my mind.

Jews had always been a strange puzzle to me. When at school I had made a special study of their history. I had delved deep into their religion on account of its occult significance. I had spent sleepless nights over the wonders of their Kabbala and yet I had always asked, why is this race the most sceptical and materialistic that can be found in the world to-day ?

Again these thoughts came to me-this race that God had taught by occultism, whose twelve tribes represented the twelve signs of the Zodiac, whose every action had been predicted in advance, whose prophets were higher than their priests, whose every letter in their Hebrew alphabet was associated with a Number and its occult meaning.

Could it be possible, I thought, that by losing the key to the occult mysteries of their own religion, they had paid the penalty by Loss loss of greatness-loss of country and the thousand and one privations they had since undergone?

When the Master of Miracles, the despised Nazarene, whose every step was the fulfilment of a prediction, showed them the wonders of nature's occult forces, even then their scepticism blinded them to the truth-and so the " chosen race," before whom the walls of Jericho (by reason of their obeying the occult law of Seven) fell, became the byword of the world.

I had of ten wondered why they were called "God's chosen people," and as there is no statement in Holy Writ that has not its own peculiar message, I had come to the conclusion that they were "chosen" as the race through whom the Creator manifests the occult meaning of humanity.

They were the children of Destiny, preaching unconsciously the purpose of God to all people, and the living proof of design in all the happenings of the past-the present-and the to be.

At the commencement of history their seven days or periods of creation corresponded in the most absolute degree to the rule of the seven creative planets that were given to control this earth and carry on its destiny.

First, was the cycle of the Sun, the period when science tells us that the earth was a mass of molten fire, being moulded for a future purpose, when "the light was divided from the darkness."

Second, the cycle of the Moon, when the "waters were divided" and since when the moon controls the world's tides.

Third, the cycle of Mars-when the "dry land" was made appear and vegetation burst forth and energy and force, symbols of Mars, were first felt throughout the earth.

Fourth, the period of Mercury, symbolic of the science of the stars "from which all science comes," the period in which He "set the planets in the firmament of heaven to rule over the day and over the night."

Fifth, the cycle of Jupiter, the creation of the spirit of restlessness and desire in nature which is in itself the symbol of Ambition.

Sixth, the cycle of Venus, the period of the creation of animals and humanity itself, "male and female created He them," and symbolising that the highest stage of animal and human progression is the creation of the human species, for whose special purpose everything else was made.

Seventh, the cycle of Saturn, emblematic of rest, reflection and death (as God "rested on the seventh day and hallowed it").

As the world was built up by these seven creative planets, so do they in their turn continue to hold their sway over all creation.

Later on in the history of the world, Christ himself died on the evening of " the sixth day of the week "-the last of the working days that the Creator had appoi'nted at the beginni'ng of thi'ngs. Further He lay in the tomb in the repose of death during the seventh day, the day that even at the beginning, the Creator had said, "no man shall work."

"On the first day of the week," "at the breaking of the day," again fulfilling the occult meaning of the seven creative planets, and at the very moment on that day which symbolises the Sun, Christ himself, called the " Sun of Righteous ness," rose from the darkness of the Tomb, even as the Ruler of our Solar System rose at the same moment from the shadows of the night.

And so it was with the Jews; they were "chosen " to be the example of these truths. Their very Temple was built "from the pattern showed them in the Heavens"; they had even the Shekinah with them until they closed their eyes to its light and drove themselves out into the darkness, to wear on their faces the brand of scepticism that even the simplest reader of character may read.

They have sold their birthright, namely, the glorious occult truth of their grand religion, for the world's "mess of pottage"; and their priests have lost the keys of the Tabernacle that the great Jews their fathers had before them.

They hope for the Messiah to come, but they little think that when he does come it will be to teach them the occult truths of their own religion, and the first lesson they will learn will be that they were "chosen" to be an example unto others of the laws of Destiny that rule worlds, nations and individual lives.

Such thoughts as these were teeming trough my mind, when I felt a touch on my shoulder and saw the Jew I had passed standing at my side.

"What, you don't remember me ? " he said.

" I cannot say I do," I replied.

"Well," he answered, "I have reason to re member you. You read my hands in Egypt and the things you told me happened, even down to my divorce case last month."

"Well then, you believe in the study now, I suppose?"

"Oh, no, I don't," he said. "I can't believe in such things, but there's money in it, my friend. You ought to make a fortune. Are you doing it now, I want some friends to see you?"

"No," I said, "I am doing nothing; at least, only some writing for papers."

He laughed. "It's only fools who write," he said, and before I could collect my thoughts he already had a glittering proposition placed before me,

We walked round to his office-on the walls were some musty old paintings, on the table bits of china, some Egyptian scarabs and a bust of Grecian marble. He was a Government official, but he made money by anything he could lay his hands on.

Half an hour later I went back into the street, having signed a contract with him to commence at once in London, which contract, by the way, bound me to give him fifty per cent of all the money I made for twelve years from that date.

Still one must give him credit for his enterprise.

CHAPTER IV

THE CHOICE OF A NAME : AN ACT OF PARLIAMENT : THE CONTRACT BROKEN

THE same day I started out with new found courage to find suitable rooms to work in, in the West-end.

But to find rooms was not an easy matter.

In those pre-palmistic days Palmistry was an " unknown and unheard-of quantity" in London.

It was an art relegated to gypsies and associated in the minds of landlords with everything that was evil. It was sufficient to mention the purpose for which I wanted the premises to receive a stern refusal and in some cases a religious lecture on tampering with such works of the devil.

At last I discovered a Scotch landlady (another race whose shrewdness I have since respected nearly as much as I do that of the Jews).

She was a good Catholic with a small purse and a consumptive husband, but on my agreeing to pay double the rent, she arranged the affair with her conscience.

But the conscience of a Scotch woman is not a thing so easily lulled to sleep. I soon found she sprinkled holy water night and morning at my door, and on moving to larger premises a month later she charged me heavily for damage done to the carpet.

I was installed, it was true, but another difficulty cropped up; I had no name to work under, for as my father was still living, I would not take my own. My Jew friend and myself discussed the question day after day. Biblical names he suggested by the dozen, and at one moment he was particularly keen on a nom de guerre of "Solomon," but, fortunately for me, he had had that name applied to himself in that recent divorce case on account of his emulation of that monarch's desire to study the book of wisdom called "Woman," so he finally decided such a distinguished name was too risky for so young a man as myself.

As the days went and no name was found he began to get impatient at what he called my "capricious fancy."

He quoted Shakespeare's opinion on names every time we met, and wrote long letters on "procrastination the thief of time," the "great ness of opportunity" and so forth, and yet when the right name did come, he was the last man in London to acknowledge it.

One night, more worried than usual by his reproaches, my tired brain dreamt of names by hundreds, till suddenly I seemed to see in Greek and English the name "CHEIRO" standing out before me.

The next morning I announced my discovery.

He repeated the name over and over again, and then informed me that I was a fool, that no one could pronounce it, that it had no meaning and was useless.

In vain I explained that Cheir was the Greek word for hand, and that "Cheiro " would thus become identified by intelligent people with the exponent of the hand.

" Fool I " was the only answer he deigned to give, and fearing" Solomon" might be again revived, I rushed to the nearest printers and so the name" CHEIRO" became launched.

In a few weeks clients began to come regularly and at the end of the first month my Hebrew friend received back whatever money he had advanced, together with the fifty percent, he had bargained for.

He was extremely happy over what he was pleased to call "his occult investment."

His happiness, however, was not fated to last long. One afternoon he rushed up in a very excited state and thrust an evening paper under my eyes. "Look there," he said, pointing to a paragraph; "I shall be ruined."

Looking down the column I found that some reporter in writing about the vogue I had started in London, quoted, to show his extreme learning on the subject, an extract from an old Act of Parliament to prove that all such professions were nothing less than illegal.

The Act in question had been made in the time of Henry the VIII., probably because the " Merry Monarch" did not desire that his many wives should have any chance to find out their unhappy fate by such aids as Astrology or Palmistry.

This intelligent Act of Parliament read as follows:

"Any person or persons found guilty of practising Astrology, Palmistry, Witchcraft, or all such works of the devil, is hereby deemed a rogue and a vagabond to be sentenced to lose all his goods and possessions, to stand one year in the pillory, to be expelled from the country, or to be imprisoned for life."

After the passing of such an Act it is to be hoped that the "much married monarch" slept in peace, knowing that Anne Boleyn or Catherine Howard would be safe from learning their future by "such works of the devil."

History also states that the King blamed Astrology for the rebellion of the Duke of Buckingham, but whether it was caused by wives or rebellions, in any case this intelligent Act had come into force. Under Elizabeth it fell into abeyance, due, perhaps, to her belief in the famous old astrologer, John Dee, and her many visits to consult him at Mortlake.

In any case history tells us that this great old Astrologer, Mystic, and Palmist, acted for over twenty years as the Queen's Adviser and counsellor, and who knows if the greatness of England to-day does not owe more than any one may imagine to "Queen Bess" acting on the advice given her from such occult studies as old John Dee was master of at that time?

Under George III., whose name is also handed down to posterity for the loss of America, the old Act was revived; and as times may change and people may change but Acts of Parliament never, so this intelligent law remains to the present day, and had the effect of frightening my Hebrew friend out of his seven senses.

"My dear boy," he said, " I shall be ruined. I am a Government official. I shall retire with a pension in a few years. I shall lose all if I am found aiding and abetting a person to break an Act of Parliament. You have paid me back my money with interest, for Heaven's sake tear up the contract and burn it and if you get into trouble never mention my name or that you ever knew me."

Within five minutes the contract was burned, we shook hands, and I was again free man.

CHAPTER V

AFTER the contract with my Hebrew friend was broken up, people came more and more to hear what I had to say. One person recommended me to another and so things went on for the first few months.

One afternoon a very imperious mother with a beautiful daughter came. The imperious mother had in her own mind a very wonderful future mapped out for the fragile looking saint by her side. My rule, even then, was never to see two people together when giving one of my consultations-but the imperious mother would not hear for a moment of any such arrangement.

"What is society coming to," she shrieked, "to allow a young girl to be alone in a man's company for half an hour?"

I tried to assure her that it was only the hands of her beautiful daughter which interested me, but finally I gave in and the imperious mother promised to keep quiet and not to interrupt. On this occasion I was extremely nervous, for my experience had already taught me that even the most intimate friends seldom know the real character of the person they are with, and of all people parents generally make the greatest mistakes about the characters of their own children.

The slender hands of this perfect model for a Madonna were opened on the cushion before me. I glanced for a moment on their maze of complicated lines and then back to the calm, self-possessed, beautiful face of this girl of nineteen.

I made the one mistake. I though(the mother knew what anxiety and trouble that girl was passing through even then, and that she had perhaps come to me for advice as to how she might best help her, and believing that, rapid as words could come to me, I drew the picture of her wrecked life, the broken marriage she had already made, and the disgrace that seemed already surrounding her. Pity seemed to choke me and I stopped. It was well I did, for in another second I think the imperious mother would have had a fit of apoplexy. As I saw her angry, purple face, I knew the mistake I had made in speaking as I had done, and I hardly dared to meet the girl's eyes.

Drawing on her gloves in the calmest way she said:

" Mother, what a fraud this person is I " and for a moment I really thought I was.

Then the storm broke and the imperious mother told me what she thought of both myself and my art, and like an angry whirlwind swept out of the place.

I was completely unnerved for the day. I knew I had not made a mistake, but I realised what a disastrous advertisement I would get from these visitors. At every house where the mother called, at every reception she attended, she repeated to every one what I had said-and then one morning the denouement came. This poor girl, this wonderful actress, was arrested for cashing a forged cheque. She had been married for two years to a scoundrel. He got out of the country, and left her to get on as best she could.

We met again years later, and I am thankful to say I was able to be of some considerable assistance to her.

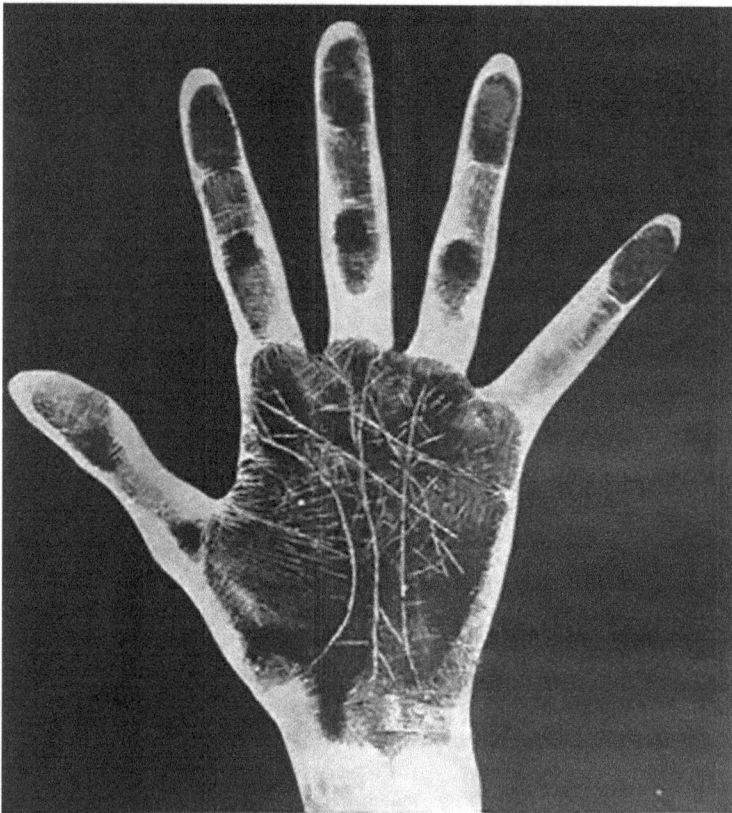

MADAME SARAH BERNHARDT'S RIGHT HAND

Note the two strongly marked lines from the wrist to the second and third fingers

CHAPTER VI

LONDON talked after this, of course, and my time became so taken up that people had to book appointments even weeks in advance, and then came a curious adventure, which I shall always remember with pleasure. One evening a gentle man drove up and asked if I would drive out with him and meet a lady whose hands he thought would be of great interest to me. I agreed and together we went to a house standing in a large garden near St. John's Wood. I had been made to promise to ask no questions, but I must con fess I was somewhat anxious when, after what appeared to me a considerable time, the door at the end of a corridor opened, and a lady with a heavy, black lace mantilla covering her head and face came towards me and held her hands out under a shaded electric light.

And what hands they were 1 From my point of view of lines and marks they completely fascinated me.

I scarcely knew what I said. I was keyed up to a pitch of nervousness and intensity, especially as my subject broke in every now and then with the exclamation, "Mon Dieu, comme c'est bien vrai." Then after my description of the pathway of brilliancy and success-the glory of the con quest-the triumphs and also the trials of the successful, I painted the ending of the day, the burning out one by one of the lamps of life, the slow levelling process of the hills of hope and ambition, and something else, that seemed like a tragedy-and the end.

The white hands were drawn away, great sobs came from under the veil, until suddenly it was thrown back, and the eyes of the great Sarah, those wonderful eyes, looked straight out into mine.

It is not my part in these rough sketches of the past to tell of my own feelings or of my emotions, but I must admit that at this stage of my unusual career I felt a flush of pride and gratitude to the study that had brought me so close to the only Bernhardt, especially as in the sweetest of voices my young ears had ever known she murmured over and over again in French, " It is the most wonderful thing I have ever known, wonderful, wonderful, wonderful."

But quickly I thought, the sceptical public will never believe I have seen" the only Sarah," so I handed her my autograph book and asked her to write something in it as a souvenir. Without hesitating a moment she wrote the following words and signed it with her own characteristic signature.

TRANSLATION

" Since God has placed in our hands lines and marks which tell our past and future, I only regret that from these lines we cannot know the future of those dearest to us so that we might be enabled to warn them of coming troubles or sorrows, but God doeth all things well-so be it then, Amen.

Before I left I took an impression of her hand in plaster which I published years ago in my well-known book, " Cheiro's Language of the Hand," and which I reproduce here.

As its main characteristics are so decided and clear, a short explanation may, I think, be of interest to my readers.

In the first place the shape of a hand to the student of such things should surely tell as much as the shape of the limbs of a horse to a judge of horseflesh.

To the latter every movement, every line is an indication of breeding, "form," and the like, and an experienced eye is able in a moment to "place" the horse as suitable for one class of work or the other, to tell its weak points, its strong ones, and if success or failure is likely to attend its career.

In the same way the shape of the hand to the person versed by experience in such matters shows the characteristics of the person, the heredity, breeding, peculiarities of temperament, &c., upon which the mentality will play as upon an instrument.

Surely there is nothing illogical in such reasoning. People with square-shaped, heavy hands, with square-looking, blunt fingers, are found to be methodical, solid, materialistic in their thoughts and actions, whereas those with plump, rounded hands and pointed fingers are found to be impulsive, excitable, artistic, and so forth.

The reproduction of Madame Bernhardt's cast, it will be easily seen, belongs to the latter and not to the former description.

Now glancing at the lines (which are the indication of the mentality), it has equally been found that all persons who have these straight decided looking lines have strong decided personalities which stamp all they undertake with their Will power, precision and purpose. Some may have only one line straight and clearly indicated and all the others slightly marked or wavering, and then they will be found to be decided in purpose in whatever that line represents.

In Madame Bernhardt's case, however, it will be seen that nearly all the principal lines are strangely clear and straight, and in such a case one would find that the owner must mark all she would undertake with an unmistakable personality of her own ; Madame Bernhardt's career is too well known for me to draw examples of this from the various things she has undertaken, but it is admitted that even her sculpture has always been as decided in its character as her dramatic power has been in another branch of art.

The two straight lines rising from the wrist to the second and third fingers are rarely found so clear. The one to the second finger is called the Line of Destiny, or, as I prefer to call it, the Line of Individuality, while the line to the third is called the Line of Success, or the Line of Sun, for it symbolises brilliancy, glory and success.

In some hands it is not found at all, in others it appears very broken, or wavering and uncertain, but in all cases where it appears clear and decided such people have greater brilliancy of success than others and have more light or publicity thrown on their lives.

When it is seen low down in the palm, near the wrist, the qualities above referred to will appear earlier in life than when it is only seen about the middle of the hand, or will appear later when it is seen near the root of the third finger.

Looking at these points alone, it must be admitted that this hand of the great Sarah is only in exact accordance with a career which dazzled the world even in her earlier years, and which has continued all through the brilliant pathway of her life. The centre horizontal line, lying across the middle of the palm, is called the Line of Head or Mentality.

When found as it is in her case straight and clear, it indicates, similarly to the explanation I have given of the upward lines, a strongly marked mentality-an active determined will and by lying so evenly across the palm, great versatility of talent in all which that mental will may dictate to its owner to undertake.

As the shape of the hand is, however, that of the rounded type, with tapering fingers, it is in such cases a foregone conclusion that such mentality must necessarily be used in some artistic emotional career, where such a temperament would find the more suitable conditions for its own development.

If such lines had been found in a square shaped hand with squared or blunted-looking finger-tips, then the success would have been on the contrary in some domain where a practical, scientific or methodical kind of career would have been the base.

This slight explanation will, I think, enable my readers to judge for themselves upon what a reasonable ground this strange study has been built, and how clear it can be made to those who will take the trouble to examine it from a natural standpoint apart from the superstitious and mysterious.

As Oscar Wilde wrote in my autograph book years later, "The mystery of life is the visible not the invisible."

Statue executed by The Carrara Marble Works, Regent St., W.

BLANCHE ROOSEVELT'S TOMB IN BROMPTON CEMETERY

CHAPTER VII

FATE DECIDES : MRS. WALTER PALMER'S AT HOME"

AGAIN London talked, but this time it talked too much, and so some of those newspapers whose only delight seems to be in tormenting the successful-some of those vultures of the press whom, thank God, the climate of England does not encourage-for the first time came about my door, and one or two openly threatened blackmail.

Some articles appeared again calling attention to the old Act of Parliament passed in the reign of Henry VIII. which I have referred to in a former chapter.

I was young then, I did not know the envy, hatred and unkindness of humanity. I had been for years so wrapt up and absorbed in my own particular study that the jealousy of the world was something new to me. I felt it-and felt it deeply.

One Monday morning I received two of these articles, and feeling completely discouraged I told my secretary not to make any more appointments at the end of that week, for on the following Saturday at six o'clock I intended to see my last client.

I never worked harder or did better than during that week, and at six o'clock on Saturday, as far as my plans were concerned, I had finished my career as" Cheiro."

Fate, however, who had played such an eventful part in bringing into my life actions over which I had no control, had evidently planned otherwise. I heard a lady's voice at the door entreating my secretary to arrange an interview then and there, and so the lady entered.

At the end of the interview, leaning back in her chair she said: " I shall have some very interesting people coming to my house to-night. What will your fee be to come and demonstrate your work?"

"Nothing, Madam," I said, "absolutely nothing; since six o'clock to-day 'Cheiro' has ceased to exist, but if you will allow me I will give you my services with pleasure, as I only want to convince intelligent people that there are some who carry on this study who are neither charlatans nor impostors."

"Thank you," she said, "you shall have your opportunity perhaps to-night. Here is my card, 'Mrs. Walter Palmer, Brook Street.' I will expect you at 9.30."

The guests tripped up the stairs laughing and talking-the first person they insisted on my seeing was an elderly gentleman whom they addressed

as" the doctor." "The doctor" with out opening his lips submitted fairly
gracefully to "the torture," and in a few moments I had sketched out
the main points of his career, the years in which he had made such and
such changes, &c. He became interested, the laughing ceased, and finally
when I stopped he said: " Well, I have been your greatest sceptic and have
argued all the evening against such a thing being possible, but I don't care
whether you have told me these things by my hands or by my boots, you
have certainly hit on dates and things that are accurate, and how you have
done it I do not know."

"Still," I said, "if you are a doctor this science is all wrong, for you are
no more fit to be a doctor than is the man in the moon."

" Well, sir," he said, "what profession by • my lines' should I then
have followed ?"

" Only one," I answered, "that of a barrister, or better still perhaps,
a criminal lawyer."

Pulling out his card case my visitor said, " I confess I think you really
deserve to know who I am." On the card he handed me I read the well-
known name of MR. GEORGE LEWIS.[1]

After that, one guest after the other passed through the ordeal, Mr.
Herbert Gladstone, Sir Henry Irving, Mr. Comyns Carr, and dozens of
others, until finally, at nearly 3 o'clock A.M., Mrs. Palmer said I must be
too tired to do more, and she invited me to call the next day and talk over
what she said was her triumph a well as mine.

The next day (Sunday) she said: "You-'-cannot possibly think of giving
this work up," and then I told her of the newspaper articles which had
been sent to me, of the Act of Parliament prohibiting it, &c.

In her enthusiastic way she said : "You made such a success last night
with Mr. George Lewis. I will run round and ask him his opinion. Wait
here till I come back."

I waited, and when she returned she said: "George Lewis says you are
working on such a totally different foundation from what this old Act was
intended to apply to, that you do not come under it, and if you have any
trouble you are to put your case in his hands and he will defend it for you."

The next morning I resumed my professional life, and never at any
time did I hear again of any interference or talk of this obsolete Act of
Parliament.

---

1   Afterwards Sir George Lewis.

CHAPTER VIII

Society Incidents: Blanche Roosevelt and a Meeting with Oscar Wilde: A Strange Prediction and its Fulfilment

WHEN I recommenced I decided to place my talent two days every week at the service of those who could not afford to pay my fees. I felt by so doing I was giving a part of what God had given me to His poor. For a few weeks I even had the satisfaction of believing I was doing what was right, what was charitable, until one day I realised that in this world it is as difficult to do good-as it is easy to do wrong.

I found the poor did not come, but in their place the Duchess of So-and-So, and Lady This or That, left their carriages at the corner of the next street and took up the time for nothing which I had set apart for the poor. Then in my turn I retaliated. I increased my prices, saw no person without a fee and did my charity myself.

I never, however, refused an application from any person who could not afford my fees, and every season my books showed that I gave my time to many hundreds of people for nothing.

One afternoon an unusually handsome woman called. She was my last client that day; and after she had left I mentally reviewed all I had told her. I had been unusually accurate with her, I knew, and I passed over and over again in my mind, the things I had mentioned, and the dates I had worked out for events that I thought must happen. From a peculiar system of my own, which I will explain later, in which dates, numbers and time can be worked out to such an extent that I even believe the events of every hour may be more or less indicated, it seemed to me that my late visitor would be threatened with a serious danger from fire on that very evening. Some people might probably call this a species of clairvoyance, but to my way of thinking, with certain calculations as a base, the trained and intuitive mind, due largely to concentration, is enabled to interpret the "shadows of coming events " and feel them, as even animals sometimes feel the approach of danger hours in advance.

Be this as it may. I became so convinced of this danger of fire threatening my late visitor that, in spite of a hundred reasons against my doing such a thing, I determined to see her at once and give her the warning. I bad no idea of her name, for my visitors never gave them, but when leaving she had told my servant to tell the cabman a certain well-known hotel, and so I at once proceeded there.

My description at the hotel office was sufficient; my card was sent up and she received me. At first she thought I was mad and frankly told me so, but finally she became impressed with my earnestness and agreed to leave the hotel and stop the night at the house of a friend of hers, Mrs. Charles Hawtrey of Wilton Crescent.

And now came the strange part of the story. No fire of any kind took place. But her pet dog which she left behind was during the night as phyxated by an escape of gas which occurred under the floor in this very room.

It was in this way I became acquainted with the famous and beautiful Blanche Roosevelt (Comtesse Machetta d' Algri). Blanche Roosevelt was one of those creatures that, like Halley's Comet, only pass over life's horizon once in so many hundred years.

Blanche was an American and every one loved her, from the beggar in the street to the Prince in the Palace, and every one called her Blanche, for no title seemed to adorn her more than her own simple Christian name. This strange being, a veritable spoiled child of the gods, was gifted as few women have ever been either before or since. She was an authoress and poetess of no small merit, her "Copper Queen," with its vivid picture of the Chicago fire, was considered one of the best novels of the day. She could paint as few artists could, and sing as few prima donnas.

Liszt worshipped her and encouraged her in music, while the great Sardou and Bulwer Lytton tried to draw her into the world of letters.

Apart from her talents, she had a charm of beauty and the apparent guilelessness of not knowing it that drew women to her as much as men. Even Queen Victoria after her presentation at Court had requested to see her again. If I could only sketch her you would perhaps under stand it-the whitest teeth, the fairest skin, the bluest eyes and hair like beaten gold that any artist has ever imagined, a figure divinely tall with the bearing of a queen, the grace of a thoroughbred, and with it all the simplicity of a child. Such in a few words was Blanche.

Shortly after the "fire" incident I mentioned, she gave a dinner where it was arranged that I was to read hands through a curtain so that I might not know who my consultants were. When my work was finished I was presented to the Prince Colonna, the Duke of--,Madame Melba, Lord Leighton, Henry Abbey of New York, and many others.

The greatest hit I made that evening was in the case of Oscar Wilde, who was then at the height of his fame in London. He had produced that very night "The Woman of No Importance," but I little thought when his rather fat hands were passed through the holes in the curtain that such hands could belong to the most talked of man in London at that moment.

I was however so struck with the difference in the markings of the left and right hands, that from behind my curtain I explained that the left always denoted the hereditary tendencies, while the right showed the developed or attained characteristics, and that when we use the left side of the brain the nerves cross and go to the right hand, so that the right consequently shows the true nature and development of the individual. I pointed this case out as an example where the left had promised the most unusual destiny of brilliancy and uninterrupted success, which was completely broken and ruined at a certain date in the right. Almost forgetting myself for a moment, I summed up all by saying, "the left hand is the hand of a king, but the right that of a king who will send himself into exile."

The owner of the hands did not laugh. "At what date?" he asked rather quietly.

"A few years from now," I answered, "be tween your forty-first and forty-second year."

Of course every one laughed. "What a joke! " they said, but in the most dramatic manner, Wilde turned towards them and repeated gravely, "The left is the hand of a king, but the right is that of a king who will send himself into exile," and without another word he left.

That was the end of the evening. Blanche was rather annoyed (at least as much so as she could ever be at anything) that I had sent the lion of her party away. She told me I was too realistic for drawing-room entertainments, so my curtains were taken down and supper was served instead of science.

I did not meet Oscar Wilde again until shortly before he commenced the case that was to end so fatally for him. He came then to see "if the break was still there." I told him it was, but that surely his Destiny could not be broken. He was very, very quiet, but in a far off way he said: "My good friend, you know well Fate does not keep road-menders on her high ways."

I never met him again until I had wandered half round the world and reached Paris in 1900. It was a lovely summer evening in the Exhibition. I had been dining there with friends, and as we sat on the terrace of one of the principal restaurants, a strange, gaunt, broken figure passed and took a seat far away from the crowd.

I should not have recognised him if some of our party had not exclaimed, "Why, that's Oscar Wilde l" Instinctively I rose. "I must go and speak to him," I said.

" If you do," my host replied, " you need not return." I accepted the challenge and went to Wilde and held out my hand.

In his terrible loneliness he held it for a moment and then burst into tears.

"My dear friend," he said, "how good of you! Every one cuts me now. How good of you to come to me ! "

And then we talked-talked till the music ceased, till the sound of voices and passing feet grew silent and the great Exhibition wrapt itself into gloom.

He went through the trial again-the mistakes he had made, the life in the prison, the joy of liberty-all. And then he told me the bitterest part of all, the hopelessness of despair, of the slights and cuts by old friends and the impossibility of getting back into his place in the world again the reading of a blood.

He passed all in review like human document written in blood.

It was no use offering him comfort or hope his brain was too great to feed on dreams-it was awake to the terrible reality of life, to the cruel truth that Fate for him was broken.

Suddenly after an outburst of words where foam and froth and depth like a mighty torrent of language tore down the banks of conventionality, the river seemed to give him an idea, and in a second he was at its side. As he stood on the parapet the moon shone out and outlined every curve of the massive, broken figure that seemed about to plunge into the quiet river at his feet.

I reached his side and clutched his arm, but he as suddenly turned, and with the most satirical laugh I have ever heard, said, "No, my boy, they shall not say that Oscar took his own life. How the dogs would yelp and the press would ring with their graphic descriptions I They have hounded me enough, God knows, but to-night has given me the courage to face them, and the pain-and the death-that is every day coming nearer. If you never did a kind action in your life you did one to-night by coming to me with your sympathy and your friendship.

You have walked in the Valley of the Shadow with me the Gethsemane of life that all pass through sooner or later.

I am glad the test has come, and is over.

"Your presence brought the dead past out of its grave. You remember that night at Blanche's the very night on which I had made one of my great triumphs, and you remember what you told me. How often I have thought of it since, and while I picked oakum I often looked at my hands and wondered at that break so clearly shown in the mark of Fate, and also wondered why I was unable to take the warning.

"You have done me good to-night. You have brought me back to myself. Now let me walk home alone through the quiet streets. We shall surely meet again in this great village of Paris." We never met again but I was one of the few who followed his coffin to the grave a few months later.

CHAPTER IX

D URING 1891 I had the honour of meeting, for the first time, the late King Edward, under the following circumstances.

One of my clients, a distinguished lady, well known in Society, had invited me to call at her house in Mayfair on a certain evening, after dinner. When I arrived she met me in the hall and took me to the smoking-room at the end of the passage.

"Now," she said, "I want you to do me a great favour. I want you to sit behind these curtains that I have fixed up, and read as clearly as you can the hands of a man who is coming here expressly for this purpose."

" You will be alone with him and you are to say frankly what you see without having any regard for his feelings. Now, you will do your utmost, will you not ? "

" Certainly," I said, "I will do the best I can." I went behind the curtains, arranged an electric light so that I might be able to see the hands in question to the best advantage, and then waited for my "subject" to appear.

In a few moments she returned accompanied by a gentleman, and having fixed his hands through the curtains she left us together.

Little thinking who the visitor was I went ahead with the same composure as I would have done with any one of my daily consultants.

My "subject" seemed to enjoy the experience immensely; once or twice he asked some question and occasionally he withdrew his hands to make notes, and so we went on until I began to indicate the important years in the destiny for certain changes and events which seemed beyond his control.

I had got to the point of telling how and why the most important days every week for him would be Tuesdays, Thursdays, and Fridays, and that his important numbers were sixes and nines, and that the months which represented these numbers, being March 21 to April 21, April 21 to May 27, and October 21 to November 27, would contain the most important events concerning him personally.

"Strange," he said, "but that is remarkably true."

Just then he leaned on the curtain a little too much, and, as ladies are not famous for fastening things securely, the pins came out-the curtains dropped at our feet-and I found myself sitting face to face with the then Prince of Wales.

I must have looked frightened out of my wits, for in the kindest possible way he said, "You have no need to be nervous, you have done splendidly, and it is the first time in my life that I have had genuine satisfaction with this kind of thing. Go on with this curious idea of numbers that you have got; forget who I am and be just as much at your ease as you were before."

His gracious manner would have made even the most nervous person calm ; so, pulling up a table and getting some paper, I worked out by my system a diagram, showing when the most important events of his life would happen, and with what exactness they would fall into certain months of the year and not into others.

We quietly worked it out, and he himself pointed out the number 69, and said: "As this is the only date when these two curious numbers which you say are the key-notes of my life come together, I suppose then that must be the end."

How far off it seemed, and yet he himself with strange exactness had picked out the fadic date![2]

By this system of numbers the month of April, the month in which he caught his last illness, has from time immemorial been represented by the number 9.

The month of May in which he died is represented by a 6.

The very addition of the age, 69, by natural addition gives 6 + 9 = I 5 ; 1 + 5 = 6. He passed away on a 6th of May, a Friday, which is also in the most ancient writings on this system of calculation represented by the number of 6.

THE SECOND MEETING

Years later I had again the honour to meet him when he was still Prince of Wales, but under very different conditions.

The Boer War had just broken out, and thou sands of British soldiers were leaving by every ship for South Africa.

The Princess of -,   who had enjoyed from her childhood the friendship of the Prince of Wales, had come to London with a very clever plan for sending cargoes of biscuits out to the soldiers.

She had enlisted the interest of the Prince in her idea, and as she had implicit confidence in me she had enrolled me in her scheme for getting options from the big biscuit manufacturers of England, as she had already done on the Continent.

One afternoon in her sitting-room in the Berkeley Hotel, I was actively engaged in placing before her the details of the options I had been able to secure, when some one knocked at the door and the Prince of Wales entered.

---

2   King Edward was in his sixty-ninth year when he died.

She was about to present me when the Prince laughed and said, "Why, this is the man who will not let me live past sixty nine."

"What a pity you are not the Kaiser," she answered, "he would already have been executed for lese Majeste."

Alas ! for her plan. The Prince had taken the trouble to come and tell her that he had just heard from the War Office that they had discovered large stores of biscuits that had not been thought of before and that several cargoes of them were already ordered to the front.

A few evenings later I chanced to meet the Prince leaving the Marlborough Club. Coming towards me he said: "I would like to have another chat with you about your theory of Numbers, come with me to my library where we shall not be disturbed."

Together we entered Marlborough House. First handing me a cigar and then some paper he asked me to work out "the Numbers" of different people whose birth dates he mentioned, and from six o'clock until nearly eight -I worked on steadily, until a message was brought to him that he had to dress for dinner.

I kept notes of the dates and questions he asked, but I do not think I am justified in making them public, or his remarks on my observations

When finally he rose to go, he shook hand with me in the most gracious manner, and the making me light another cigar he walked wit me as far as the hall, and again holding out hi hand he said "Good-bye."

Stereoscopic Company, Regent St., W.

THE LATE KING EDWARD VII IN HIS LIBRARY
AT MARLBOROUGH HOUSE

CHAPTER X

FOLLOWING the preceding account of my interview with King
Edward VII, it may not be out of place if I relate here how I was later
instrumental in helping forward his now famous project of the Entente
Cordiale between England and France, and, in fact, being, I may safely
say, one of the first promoters of the idea, at least in Paris.

I had naturally never forgotten His Majesty's condescension and kind
manner towards me, and when living in Paris shortly after the "Fashoda
affair," which excited so much French feeling against England, I did my
best in my small way to ensure that at least his name should be respected
at the various meetings and gatherings I attended.

During my earlier education one of my tutors-an old man who knew
the world well-had once said to me: "My boy, I will give you a golden rule
for Life's rough journey. It is this: 'Do good to those who do good to you;
and as for those who do you harm-be sorry for their lack of judgment.' If
you follow this rule, it may not make you a millionaire, but it will at least
give you great satisfaction."

I had never forgotten my old tutor's words; his maxim became one of
the fixed principles of my life, and I must admit I have sometimes gone
to extremes to carry it into effect.

The feeling in Paris at the time of which I am writing was so bitter
against even any one who happened to "look English" that I often saw
Americans when walking through the Boulevards hold some American
paper prominently in their hands so that the passers-by could see that,
though they spoke the language, they yet did not belong to the " hated
race of land-grabbers who had stolen Fashoda."

About this time I had purchased and become sole proprietor of the
American Register and Anglo-Colonial World, a newspaper that had
been founded during the last years of the Empire and which had the
distinction, as it still has to-day, of being the oldest paper published in
English on the Continent.

As this newspaper was so well known and so respected by French
people for the impartiality of its politics and its continuous efforts to pro
mote a good understanding between the Latin and Anglo-Saxon races, I
conceived the idea that it might be employed in some way to over come
the bad feeling already mentioned.

I had remarked, like so many others, that although King Edward as a man was well liked and his former visits were continually commented on, yet when classed collectively with "perfidious Albion" he bore quite another aspect.

It therefore came into my mind that it might be a good idea to collect together the views of the principal political leaders and public men as to what in their opinion would be the reception that King Edward would have if he should visit Paris at that moment.

In pursuit of this plan I caused a letter to be sent out from the American Register which, to put it briefly, asked the following questions:

That, knowing the deep sympathy and profound interest that His Majesty King Edward had always shown towards France, what in their opinion would be the reception accorded to him if he should visit Paris at that period?

And if such a visit would not do much to allay the bad feeling that existed, and be the beginning of an entente, both politically and commercially to the ultimate benefit of both nations ?

Some thousands of these letters were sent out, and in a few days, and rather to my own astonishment, replies came pouring in from all parts of France.

And what replies they were, too ! Some even went so far as to write no less than eight pages of argument either for or against the idea; some replied very tersely, a mere "yes " or " no,,; while others were so abusive as to the very idea of a newspaper asking such questions at such a moment that my very hair at times almost stood on end.

The majority, however, spoke of the King himself in terms of respect and admiration, and many went so far as to say that, if such a visit were possible, they would do their utmost to make it a personal triumph for His Majesty, even though they might not be able to forget "the last action of la politique anglaise"

As Sir Edmund Monson, the then British Ambassador to France, had always been extremely cordial to me, without consulting any one I made a packet of these letters and showed them to him, and asked if he would send them on to His Majesty.

Sir Edmund, although most considerate to me, told me frankly that, with the tension and bad feeling which existed, he did not believe any good could come from my plan, and so, with my packet of letters, I returned home.

About this time I happened to be introduced to Monsieur Delcasse, who was then Minister of Foreign Affairs. He congratulated me warmly on the attitude taken up by my news paper, and from what he said, both then and at a second interview, I determined to carry out my plan and forward the letters to His Majesty myself.

I went through them very carefully, but I admit I kept back all those that were too hastily or hotly worded, and which, I am glad to say, I still have in my possession, especially as many of those who wrote them have since altered their opinions, and are to-day staunch upholders of the entente.

So that King Edward might, perhaps, re member who his correspondent was, I wrote in my letter, "Your Majesty may perhaps recall me as the man whom your Majesty said would not let you live past sixty-nine,'" and so the letters were sent off.

Nearly a month passed. I heard nothing; but meanwhile the American Register and Anglo Colonial World continued its articles and published the most important and favourable letters we had received, and special copies of these issues were sent to almost every man of note in the political world in France and England. Many of the leading French newspapers commented on the enterprise of the American Register, and quite a large number quoted the published letters and articles in their own columns.

One afternoon I received a message requesting me to call at the British Embassy, and from Sir Edmund's own hands I received the letters returned from the King, "with his thanks for the trouble I had gone to in the matter" ; and Sir Edmund added : " In the next few days you will hear that arrangements are being made for His Majesty's visit to Paris."

It would be superfluous for me to make any comment on "the visit" itself, for almost every writer and newspaper in the world has passed judgment on its far-reaching effect.

I must, however, disagree with the "glowing descriptions" given by so many of the "warm reception" accorded to His Majesty when his carriage first drove through the streets of Paris. It was anything, in fact, but a warm, or even a lukewarm, reception. It is true that the Avenue du Bois de Boulogne and the Champs Elysees were crowded with people, but they were for the most part a very silent crowd; very few even raised their hats.

Every one knew that President Loubet and the authorities were in the greatest apprehension lest at any moment a counter demonstration should take place. Every precaution that could be taken for the King's safety was taken, and the police arrangements in the experienced hands of Monsieur Lepine were perfection itself. Still, all this could not arouse the enthusiasm of the people-a people who rather imagined that "the visit" was just" another proof how France had been sold into the mesh of perfidious Albion."

THE LAUNCHING OF THE "ENTENTE CORDIALE " NEWSPAPER

About a month before "the visit," as it became called in Paris, I thought I would follow up the success of the letters previously mentioned by starting another newspaper whose title would be more in accordance with political interests, and with this view I founded a paper called the Entente Cordi'ale, or, as its sub heading announced it," A Journal in the Interest of International Peace."

For this purpose I engaged correspondents in the principal capitals of Europe and several editors capable of carrying out its programme. All went well until the evening before we went to press with the first number, when an episode took place which was perhaps in itself an omen of the difficulties that beset the path of those who, in a world of strife, allow themselves to dream of peace.

This incident, although amusing enough now to look back upon, yet, at the moment it occurred, almost prevented the birth of the journal and nearly altered my own ideas on the feasibility of the enterprise.

On account of the errors made in the English part of the paper by our French compositors, we were compelled at the last moment to make the first issue of the publication through our London offices, and so I rushed over from Paris the night before hoping to find everything in readiness for the press.

My principal editor was an Englishman who had lived the greater part of his life on the Continent, and who was thoroughly conversant with several foreign languages. With his majestic white beard he looked in himself a perfect model for a statue of Peace, but at heart he was an incarnation of a thorough British bull dog who showed his fighting blood in a second if England's dignity or righteousness was ever called in question.

Another editor was a Frenchman who, although in !he end one of the greatest defenders of the " Entente Cordiale," yet at that time was still "a little sore over Fashoda," and always ready to bring the question up at the most inopportune moment.

The editorial staff in London was completed by an Irishman who had been a war-correspondent for the past thirty years.

The Irishman, I need hardly add, was the "powder magazine" of the ship.

His faults may have been many, but he was one of the most brilliant writers it has ever been my lot to meet. No subject was amiss to his rapid pen. International law to the history of an Egyptian mummy-all came the same to him if an article was required at the last moment, provided that one did not.... question certain generous allowance of alcohol that "was necessary," he said, "in order that his brain might see things in their proper light."

In such a combination his Irish sense of humour was, however, a somewhat serious drawback. In fact, he thought " International Peace " such a huge joke that he nearly split his sides with laughter the first time he saw our ambitious sub-title.

On the night in question, as I jumped out of my cab, even at the street door the sounds of discord and strife already reached my ears. "What's the matter?" I said to the porter. With a significant grin he replied: "It's the first night of the peace journal upstairs, sir; that's all."

Quite enough for me, I thought, but at that moment there came an appalling crash of glass, and the Frenchman came tearing down the stairs like a madman.

In the editorial room it looked as if an American cyclone had paid a surprise visit proof sheets were flying in every conceivable direction, my venerable editor had a nose so damaged that it spouted blood like a water-cart, while my ex-war-correspondent looked as if "he • had just returned from the front."

I never knew exactly what had happened for I never asked. "A good beginning," was all the Irishman said as he seized a pen and began to dash off his special article. " England," at the other end of the table, tried to look dignified ; while a diligent office boy gathered up the proofs and solemnly laid them before me.

Not a word was said, but for the few hours that followed I must confess no two men ever worked harder in their lives, with the result that some of the finest articles on the virtues of peace were produced that were perhaps ever written on the subject.

The next day the Entente Cordiale appeared on the bookstalls, and I found that we had had the honour of giving the King a new title-that of"Edward the Peacemaker." The first time he was ever called by this name was in the columns of the first issue of this journal.

In less than two months the Entente Cordiale was selling well in all parts of the world, and letters of congratulation poured in from the most unexpected quarters. Nearly every monarch in Europe wrote to acknowl-edge copies, and from far-distant Japan the Mikado sent the expresion of his best wishes for its success.

Financially there was, however, nothing I ever undertook that ended in such a balance on the wrong side. Printed on the best paper, well illustrated, and too well edited, its cost of production every month over-whelmed its income, so that after running this paper for a little over a year I was glad to stop my experiment in "the interests of peace "-and pocket a very heavy loss for my pains.

And the inconsistency of it all I While all nations praised peace they all actively prepared for war. A certain millionaire, who gets the greater part of his fortune from the manufacture of cannon and armour-plate for battleships, gave large donations to build a Palace of Peace, but no· one ever thought of supporting a journal dedicated to its propaganda. Diplomatists were the very last who ever paid their subscriptions, and when they did-it was with a request that their picture might be published in the next issue.

In the end I came to the conclusion that my Irish ex-war-correspon-dent's joke had not been far wrong, and that in the great game of politics the superb ideal of International Peace is a dream only to be indulged in-by the very rich-or the very foolish.

Before I conclude my humble remarks on this question of International Peace, I feel I must add-even at the risk of displeasing those of my readers who clamour for the curtailing of Britain's Navy-that it is Britain alone who to-day has the peace of the entire world in her keeping. It is only those who like myself have lived for many years beneath the Flags of other Nations, who can realise what England's power for Peace really means. In a menace of War there is only one question asked : "What will England do?" and it is on the answer to that vital question that all depends.

People who do not think-and they are so many-prattle " of the greatness of ancient Empires," but no Babylon, or Greece, or Rome, ever dreamt of the world-wide sway of modern Britain.

Mysterious Britain I fusion of four races English, Irish, Welsh, and Scotch-the Mother of Parliaments, and to-day the Peacemaker to all.

Yes, I have used the word Britain advisedly, for I have so often heard   the "makers of Empire " out in some far off sun-dried land, reply almost unconsciously, but perhaps also from that strange natural instinct that is the genius of all greatness: "Oh no, I am Scotch," "Irish," or "Welsh," as the case might be but with a touch of pride they have invariably added, "But I am a British subject."

Ah! if those who sit in "the chairs of State" could only hear them they would long ago have added to Britain's emblem the four-leaf sham rock-that symbol of luck and power that the so-called superstitious search for and which in ages past England found.

He is a clever man who can make others work for him, but he is still more clever if he can take all the credit and at the same time manage that the helpers are glad that he does so.   The responsibility for John Bull's government he usually puts in the hands of some man of a different nationality to his own, perhaps a Hebrew like Disraeli, a Welshman like Lloyd George, or a Scotchman like Gladstone, Camp bell-Bannerman, or Balfour. He generally ha some contented Jew to advise him about Finance an Irishman to look after his Army, and a the present moment a considerable quantity of American blood gives energy to the veins of the First Lord of his Admiralty. Above all floats hi "Union Jack," for above all others it is John Bull who has proved that it is indeed "Union that gives strength."

Surely if one thinks of these things one can only be filled with wonder for that symbolic personage whose subjects toil for his honour every land and clime, whose ships float on ever sea, whose strength is the safety of those who are weaker, and who to-day has the still proud position of being the Arbitrator of Peace among the Nations of the Earth.

CHAPTER XI

ONE of my valued souvenirs is a letter from the present Queen, at that time the Princess May.

I received this letter in the following manner. It had been commonly rumoured in London that prior to her engagement to the Duke of Clarence, Princess May, accompanied by another lady, had been to see me, and that I had stated that she would be engaged to two brothers, that her first fiancé would not live, but that through her marriage to his brother she would finally occupy a position of the very greatest power and highest responsibility.

Also that her "lucky number" was a 3 and that number would be associated with all the great events in her destiny.

As I seldom, if ever, knew the names of my visitors, I can only give this story as it was commonly rumoured and also told me by a lady who was intimately connected with the Princess May, and it was this lady who later suggested to me, when the marriage arranged with the Duke of York was announced, that I should send as a wedding present my book on hands, which had just been published.

Acting on this lady's advice I had a special copy printed, bound in white calf and gold, which I sent to White Lodge, about a fortnight before the marriage.

To my astonishment and delight the same day that the book reached its destination, I received the following gracious acknowledgment which Her Royal Highness sent me by hand, by Madame Bricka, who also told me how much the Princess had appreciated my simple gift,

WHITE LODGE,
EAST SHEEN,
May 21, 1893
"The Princess May acknowledges with many thanks Cheiro's book which he so thoughtfully sent her. She will be most happy to accept it and will place it among her wedding presents."

Referring back to the number 3, King George was born on a 3, namely June 3. The marriage of the Princess May took place in a year the addition of whose numbers makes a 3, I 893=21;

2 + I = 3, and her Coronation as Queen of England in 1911 =12 = 3 took place in a year whose "occult number" is also a 3.

I could relate many other curious things that the numbers influenc-

W. & D. Downey, 57 Ebury St., S.W.

HER MAJESTY QUEEN MARY

ing our present King and Queen indicate, but as I think they would be considered too technical for the present book I have reserved them for a work I am writing on the Book Significance of Numbers. I only hope that the strange events indicated by the years 1912[3] and 1916 will not <u>personally affect</u> England's much beloved Sovereigns.

3   In justice to the author the Publishers wish to state that the above sentence was already set up and in page form in the summer of 1911.

CHAPTER XII

Some Interesting Personalities : Mr. W. T. Steap : Miss Maup Gonne : Mr.
Richard Croker or Tammany Hall: Mlle. JANOTHA

ABOUT this time I was invited by Mr. W. T. Stead to call and see him in his well-known offices at Mowbray House.

I must here explain that in all cases when I knew who my subject was I considered myself at a great disadvantage, and for this reason I had made a rule with my secretary at my rooms that should he know the name of my intended visitor he was on no account to tell me.

My idea was (and I believe my readers will agree with me) that the brain in an ordinary way is carried away with the thought that such and such a person will lead such and such a life or do such and such a thing. The exact reverse is, on the contrary, more often the case, because men and women on life's stage play more or less of a role, while their real character is often extremely different from what it appears to the general public.

For this reason I never cared to interpret the lives of those I knew intimately, and I often dis appointed my friends by refusing even to look at their hands.

It was thus I felt on going to see Mr. Stead. He was one of those big personalities, with the limelight of public opinion playing so strongly on every action that even the " man in the street " had heard of his character in a dozen different ways through the columns of every newspaper in England.

I explained my difficulty to him ; he thought it was logical and reasonable, and so I contented myself with taking an impression of his remarkable hand for my collection and explaining to him the meaning of the difference of the lines as shown in his hand and those of other well known personalities.

Years later, however, we met in Paris, and as I was wearing the decoration which had been given me by the Shah of Persia on account of my having predicted the ate of his attempted assassination, and thus caused his Grand Vizier to ask for a stronger guard of police which, as may be remembered, saved the Shah's life, Mr. Stead made me explain how I worked out by my theory of numbers what might be called fadic dates. We were sitting at a table in a well-known restaurant in the Boulevard des Capucines, Mr. Stead, the famous Miss Maud Gonne, and my self.

Mr. Stead had returned from his visit to the Czar over his great

Peace Movement, and Miss Gonne, who was called by Parisians " the Irish Jeanne d' Arc," had just come back from one of her brilliant "peace-breaking" tours in Ireland.

When I had finished explaining my reasons for picking out the date of the attempt on the Shah's life, Mr. Stead made me tell him some things about the characters of people whose numbers, according to my system, were "keys" to their character and the chief events of their life. When I had finished he told me that the numbers he had given me were those of his own sons, and as far as he could judge, the picture I had made was exact to even the smallest details of character, and some ten years later I had the satisfaction of hearing from him that even the events which I had indicated at that dejeuner in Paris had also been fulfilled.

MR. RICHARD CROKER OF TAMMANV HALL

Later on I believe I was indebted to Mr. Stead for a meeting I had with another of those strongly marked personalities whose name is almost as well known in England as in America. I allude to Mr. Richard Croker, the then famous Leader of Tammany Hall, New York, the Chief of a political organization without its equal in the world.

After the interview he told me that he had heard "his friend Mr. Stead speak of me," and so he wanted to see what I could tell him. Strange to say, what I had told him was the very thing which at that time seemed the most unlikely to happen. He was at the moment the active Head of Tammany Hall, but I had told him that he was even then "at the parting of the ways," about to relinquish his command to another, and to exchange his active political life for one of quietness and peace. He had evidently no intention of doing so, but not more than a year later he surprised every one by retiring, buying an estate in Ireland, where subsequently he bred the winner of the Derby and won the blue ribbon of the English Turf.

MADEMOISELLE JANOTHA

Another interesting personality, of a totally different type, whom I met about this time was Mademoiselle Janotha, the famous Court Pianist to the Emperor of Germany, a lady who has received, perhaps, more decorations and honours from Royalties than perhaps any other woman in the world of music.

This weird little lady (for if one has ever heard her wonderful playing one is inclined to believe that the spirits of the great dead play through her subtle fingers) came accompanied by her famous black cat, "Prince White Heather," rolled up in her muff.

En passant, I must remark that "Prince White Heather" has been Mademoiselle's Mascot for many years, and may be seen with his mistress at all those bazaars where this generous-hearted little lady will be found working in the cause of charity.

Her great talent was so distinctly marked in the lines of her hand that I could make no mistake about it, and the following week I had the pleasure at the old St. James's Hall of being one of a large audience, who were carried away by enthusiasm at her rendering of some difficult pieces from Chopin's and Liszt's great works. It may interest my readers to hear that this great artist played over three hundred times at this famous house of music, and as a special mark of appreciation she was asked to play at the last concert before the old St. James's was demolished, and the handsome iron crown which had capped the summit of the structure for forty-seven years was presented to Mlle. Janotha as a souvenir.

A good many years have passed since then, but lately, on my return to London, I received a few lines of welcome from her, adding, "every thing you told me came true-the sorrows as well as the joys."

CHAPTER XIII

I WAS often visited by a very courteous elderly French gentleman who seemed peculiarly interested in _my system of Numbers, and more especially in some maps I had made showing the dates of the important events in the lives of the World's great personalities, such as the principal Kings of France, and diagrams relating to the battles of Napoleon the First and Wellington.

These latter diagrams he used to ask for nearly every time he came.

Napoleon's strongest period was clearly shown running from July 1 to October 30 and from January 1 to April 30, while Wellington's was from April 15 to July 15, and from October 15 to January 15.

The first time these two great generals met face to face was at Waterloo, and as this deciding battle took place on June 18, 1815, it therefore happened in Wellington's strongest "period" and Napoleon's weakest one, and this elderly gentleman used of ten to speculate as to the result to Europe generally had Napoleon been guided by a similar chart and so delayed this decisive battle until he passed into his "period."

French history my elderly visitor knew to his finger tips, and he was particularly strong on the dates of the various dynasties, revolutions, &c., but I never had the slightest idea who he was until just before my leaving London for America when I asked him if he would give me an impression of his hand as a souvenir.

"No," he replied, "for reasons of my own I do not wish to do that, but instead I shall be pleased to give you a small photo of myself which I happen to have with me." Taking out his pocketbook he produced a small carte de visite photo and going to my desk wrote his name across the bottom of the card.

When he had gone I turned to my desk and found he had signed the photo, Philippe, Comte de Paris.

MRS. LANGTRY

I never knew that Mrs. Langtry, who after wards became Lady de Bathe, had ever consulted me until some years later when she invited me to tea in her suite of rooms in the Carlton.

I asked her then if she would like me to examine her hand, to my

LADY DE BATHE
(Mrs. Langtry)

surprise she burst out laughing and said, "I had it done by you years ago. I came to you with such a heavy black veil that you could not see the tip of my nose, much less know whom you were talking to.

" It is for that reason I believe in your work, for you told me perfectly all about myself, not as the world thinks I am but as I know myself." How well I remember her that afternoon, with her charming sitting room filled with beautiful La France roses.   She was looking so radiant, so happy.

While we were talking a large box containing a handsome silver ink-stand and a sweet friendly letter of good wishes for her birthday arrived from King Edward. She had quite forgotten what day it was, but with the late King's usual thoughtfulness he had remembered it, and I feel sure that no present he ever gave brought more pleasure than did this one, on the occasion I refer to.

Before I left she presented me with the excellent photograph which I reproduce here, but those who have had the privilege of meeting Mrs. Langtry will agree with me that no picture ever did her justice or gave the faintest idea of her wonderful charm of manner or that kindliness of heart that made those who really knew her so devoted to her. I recently received the following letter from Lady de Bathe, and, as it is an instance of that kindliness of nature which I have mentioned,

I believe it will be of interest to include it in these records :

28 REGENT'S COURT,

HANOVER GATE,

April 15, 1911.

MY DEAR "CHEIR0",

I have heard that you have returned to London, and I think it is only fair to tell you how very accurate your remarks were in my case, and the strange fulfilment of what you said would happen during the past ten years.

You told me then I would not be accompanied by my husband to America, although I had planned my tour there expressly for that purpose.

I could not see how your words could come true, but the Boer War broke out and events happened exactly as you said they would.

You foretold a scandal and trouble for me in the States during the tour I was then contemplating. In this I again doubted your accuracy, as I was taking an excellent company and a play that had been a great London success. But you were again right, for I reached America during a politi-cal campaign, and the play in question, "The Degenerates," by Sydney Grundy, was dubbed on account of the title immoral by those who in such a moment were glad to seize on anything to further their party interests ; but, be that as it may, I had all the trouble and scandal which you had indicated, being in some cases hounded from town to town.

But perhaps the most curious incident was the following. You told me that about the following month of July I would have an accident in connection with a horse which would cause a shock to my nervous system which would take me some time to get over. This happened when my favourite racing mare, Maluma, ridden by Tod Sloan, broke her shoulder in the race for the Liverpool Cup and had to be killed. I must confess, whether people believe it or not, that this affected me so much that it was a long time before I could get up my enthusiasm for racing again.

These are only the things that stand out more clearly than others in the years that have passed since I last saw you, but in even minor details you were equally true in all you said.

I think it is only fair to write and tell you how accurate you have been.   Encouragement does us all so much good in our work.   I   f people could only realise this what much better efforts this world would be filled with.

Believe me,

Very truly yours, , (Signed) LILLIE DE BATHE,

CHAPTER XIV

I WILL not tire my readers by recounting many more of my experiences during my first year in London; suffice it to say that in the end, from over work, I became so ill that I passed nearly three months in a private Nursing Home in Devonshire Street, W. My appointment books showed that during my first season I had been consulted by no less than, on an average, twenty persons per day, and, counting three hundred days for a working year, I had given interviews to about six thousand persons, also attended "at homes" and garden-parties, where it was impossible to count the numbers that consulted me, and that out of the six thousand persons at my own rooms I had given over a thousand free consultations to those who could not afford my fee.

But I wanted to conquer new fields, so the moment I was sufficiently recovered to travel I determined to go to America, and with this object in view I found myself one morning standing on the platform of Waterloo waiting for the boat train to start.

My two doctors, Blanche Roosevelt and about half a dozen of my friends saw me off, and Blanche at the station presented me to Madame Nordica, who was also crossing by the same ship.

I will not describe my voyage, for in these days of travel all voyages are much the same, and yet it was an eventful moment for me, for I was en route for the States without any letters of introduction, without knowing a person there, and knowing little or nothing of Americans.

Mentally I had said good-bye to dear old England. I was under another flag, and I have often wondered since if that little bit of bunting at the mast head has affected the thousands of other travellers from England to America as it did me. I had not thought very much of what line or ship I was going to cross by until my eyes wandered upward to the mast-head, and I saw the Stars and Stripes waving in the breeze. Instinctively I looked down to the American ship and to the large crowd of Americans that it carried, and almost unconsciously I began to analyse and note down the various little differences that make their individuality distinct from the sons and daughters of Britain. In the first place the ship was run by American enterprise, it was one of the best of the fleet owned by the American Line, and as I got into conversation with some of the pas-

MADAME NORDICA
(as Isolde)

sengers I found that there was in some cases a distinct spirit of patriotism shown by their taking passage on the S.S. Paris. Now it is a mistake to think that the Americans are aggressive in their patriotism in their own country, or that the screaming of the eagle is the only music one hears in the States; on the contrary, the American eagle is much more boisterous outside of its own territory, but at home it is rather to be deplored that there is really little of the true spirit of patriotism shown by Americans in connection with the affairs of their own great nation.

Too often English people judge their cousins across the "herring pond " by the-to say the least-rather peculiar specimens that so of ten represent the travelling American in Europe.

It is this tourist class who have probably never been outside their own country before, or for the matter of that never outside their own State, who, the moment they make a little money, determine to "do Europe," and they succeed in " doing" it in such a way that poor old Europe fairly stands aghast at what she is pleased to call "those rude Yankees." Even on that short journey from London to Southampton there was a specimen of this class wearing a tie made of the Stars and Stripes, who insisted on smoking a vile cigar, putting his feet on the cushions, and making himself generally objectionable to every one around him, but I would venture to lay a wager that in his own country the same individual would have been as docile as a new-born lamb. It is the same way with a great many English people who go to America. When I lived in the States I have been more than once heartily ashamed of the sons-and even sometimes of the daughters-of Britain who visit America and who have left just as bad an impression of what English people are as do many of the class who cross the Atlantic to "do Europe." But to return to the voyage. Before noon we were out in the Channel, and with every hour the giant vessel put on more and more speed until at last she seemed like a mail train rushing through the water and with almost as much steadiness as if she were running on rails. It was an interesting thing to sit on deck and watch the various landmarks that we reached and passed along the shore. The Isle of Wight was gay with bunting, and the Needles never looked so clear, while Bournemouth-sober, steady Bournemouth,-looked positively lively as the great ship swept by. And so from day to dark, till the stars came out and the last rock was passed, and, as one by one the voyagers went below, I watched many a fair American look back across the track of foam and kiss her hand to the white cliffs of England that were fading fast from sight.

On the following day a simple incident took place that I thought worth noting down. It was Sunday and the ship's bell rang out for church and seemed so strangely sweet upon the lonely sea that it impressed me more than any church bell has done before or since, and so like many others I went down to the service.

Whatever one's religious ideas may be one cannot but be broad-minded at sea, the sight of the ocean alone would widen one's views, and if by chance there should be a little sea-sickness corning on, well then- one does not very much care whether there is a priest in broadcloth or a Salvation Army captain talking of "the better land."

In spite of an occasional roll of the ship and one or two other little inconveniences the service was most impressively conducted by the Rev. Archdeacon Kirkby of Rye, N.Y., and the incident I thought worth mentioning was the fact that, when he came to the prayer that in the Episcopal church in America is said for the President, he paid a graceful courtesy to the country he had just left by praying for the Queen of Eng- land. Considering that we were on an American ship under the American flag, and that almost all on board were Americans, it struck me that this act of courtesy, slight as it may seem, was one worthy of being recorded.

About three days out Madame Nordica sent me a charming little note inviting me to come that evening to tea in her state room.

I found Signor Perugini the well-known tenor had also been invited, and after tea the conversation turned to my work, and Nordica asked me to see if Perugini was really going to retire into a religious life, as he was for months before planning to do.

You can imagine their incredulity when I announced that Perugini would instead within a year marry a woman in his own profession, be congratulated by all, and yet the marriage would be over before six months and in a little over a year would end by a hopeless separation.

"A little rapid even for the States," they laughed-and yet it was what actually did take place. As every one knows, he was on landing engaged to sing in Lillian Russell's Company at the Casino ; in a few months he married this beautiful Prima Donna, at that time the goddess of the American stage ; in less than six months the marriage was over, and in little over a year a separation was agreed on by this curiously mated pair.

This prediction and its fulfilment did much to make my name known in New York, but still the commencement was a very difficult affair.

CHAPTER XV

A MURDERER'S HAND AND HIS SUBSEQUENT CONVICTION

I TOOK a very fine apartment in the heart of Fifth Avenue, the most exclusive street in the city; but to make oneself known in New York, without letters of introduction and without friends, is not a very easy matter.

The opportunity came in the following way: I had almost reached the end of my courage and was seriously thinking of beating a retreat, when one afternoon a very determined lady journalist called and made the following proposition :

"I have been sent by the New York World to propose the following test to you; if you accept and are successful you will get the biggest advertisement in your life ; but if you fail or refuse it you may take the next steamer home."

" What is the test ?" I asked.

"That you read without knowing the names of the persons and without asking a question, a series of impressions on paper that we will place before you-that's all," she said; "now accept it or refuse it as you like."

"All right, I accept," I said.

"I guessed you would be just such a fool," she replied, "but it's agreed."

In a few days she called with the impressions, and took down in shorthand all that I said.

We commenced; it took the whole afternoon, from two o'clock until seven, before we had finished.

I admit I was intensely nervous; the impressions were not at all good, they were taken on smoked paper, and my inquisitor was anything but sympathetic.

My very nervousness, I believe, made me succeed; my brain screwed up to such a pitch seemed to drink in every line and formation and made mental pictures of the owners in such a way that I was able to describe their characteristics as if I had known them personally.

Then came the climax-it was about the fourth or fifth impression she put before me.

"There is something in this hand so abnormal," I said, "that I shall refuse to read it unless you can bring me the consent of the owner to tell what I see."

"We have the consent of all these people," was the reply, and she

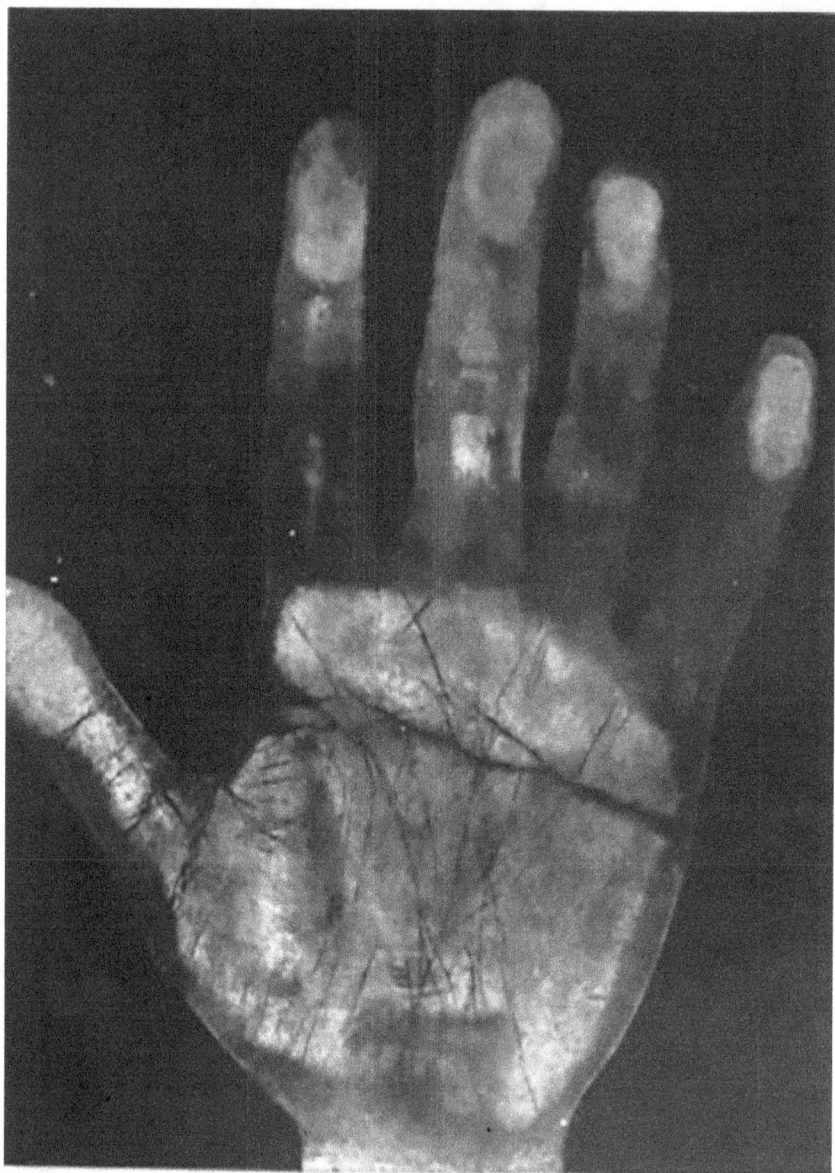

THE RIGHT HAND OF DR. MEYER, CONVICTED OF
MURDER IN NEW YORK

Note the centre horizontal line (line of mentality) across the palm
in an abnormal position, rising toward fourth finger

showed me a letter from the New York World stating that the consent had been obtained from the various persons who had given these impressions.

Under these conditions I agreed to proceed. The hand before me was that of a murderer, of that I was certain. I could make no mistake : on the left all the lines were normal and showed a high degree of intelligence-but on the right there was clear evidence that such a man had used his intelligence to obtain money by crime, and that a little over the middle of his life his very self-confidence would betray him into the hands of the law.

"Whether this man has committed one murder or twenty," I remarked, "is not the question ; at about his forty-fourth year he will be tried for murder and condemned. It will be found that for years he has used his intelligence, and whatever profession he has followed, to obtain money by crime, and that he has stopped at nothing to obtain his ends. He will be condemned, will go under the greatest strain and anxiety, will live under the very shadow of death; but his life will not end in this manner, for he will pass the remainder of his life in prison."

What really did happen was this. This man, Dr. Meyer, was convicted of insuring people's lives in Chicago-he was either their doctor or managed later to attend them-and in exercising his profession it was believed he poisoned his patients, and later collected the insurance money. At that time in the States one could insure any person, whether a relation or not, pay the premiums every year, and collect the money on the death of the individual. Since this affair occurred the law has been considerably altered.

When Dr. Meyer's case came on my prediction was fulfilled to the letter; after a long, sensational trial in which he fought every inch of the ground, he was condemned to death, but within a few days of the electrocution chair, on a technical point, the sentence was altered to imprisonment for life.

At last, when I was thoroughly exhausted, my interviewer left ; she did not give me the satisfaction of knowing whether I had been correct in my statements or not-she simply told me I would know the result in the following Sunday's World. It was then Tuesday. I lived under a very anxious strain for the following days. Saturday night I scarcely slept till near morning. About nine o'clock my black servant knocked at the door and woke me. In the most matter-of-fact way he said, "Get up, sir, there are over a hundred people sitting on the stairs waiting to see you." I did not ask the reason ; in his hand was the New York World with its entire front page devoted to the interview. I can still see the heading in big type, "Cheiro reads successfully the Lives of the Mayor, the District Attorney, Nicoll Ward McAllister, Dr. Meyer," &c.

I dressed and went out on_ the landing; the stairs were black with people of all ages, sorts and conditions.

Americans are like no other people in the world. When they take an idea into their heads they do not waste time in putting it into execution. One man made himself the spokesman, and said: "We have seen this article about you in to-day's World, and so you know now what we want."

I am told I did the right thing by replying, " I am very sorry you have taken the trouble in coming to-day, because, apart from religious scruples, I keep Sunday as a day of rest. Monday morning at nine o'clock, if you like."

I believe I rose in their eyes by my very refusal; for there is no quality Americans like more than independence.

All day long callers were told the same thing, and when Monday came my Secretary had to book appointments for nearly two months in advance.

CHAPTER XVI

A CLIENT RELATES A TERRIBLE HISTORY

I HAD many curious and exciting episodes during my first year in New York, but I will only relate a very few of them, as otherwise it would take not one, but three or four books to give the events of my American tour alone. Many of these episodes were comical, some sad beyond description, but all were more or less interesting.

Some day later I hope to write another book on my American tour, in which I shall be able to include a wider range of my experiences.

One afternoon a very carefully dressed, rather handsome man, aged about forty-five, called to see me.

As it was the busiest moment of my day I got to work at once, and spreading out this man's hands on my table, without once stopping to look up I commenced to read his past career.

I must here stop a moment to explain that though the majority of people will say that they care nothing about hearing their past, that it is their present condition which concerns them ; yet I have always found that it depends upon one's stating the past accurately whether they will have confidence in the other statements which may follow.

Besides, it will be allowed that only by building up the past can one get a clear insight into the real conditions of the consultant, and a comprehensive judgment of what the same person will do under other conditions.

It was therefore my rule always to commence with the past and give the dates when this or that event had occurred. Further, some hands are clear and comparatively easy to read, some will tell only certain things, while there are others that seem to hide the real self or the real experiences, and are more or less like masks that are difficult to penetrate; in almost all cases, however, there is some one particular thing which will stand out clear in the midst of the tangled threads of life, and which is often the key that will unlock the door of other mysteries.

With the man in question it was all ambition there was not the slightest trace of love or sentiment that had ever played a part in his career.

Starting with this key it was an easy hand to make out. The life's story could be traced as if it had been written with letters and not with lines. There was the poverty of the early life, unfortunate surroundings of the very worst, impossible, one would almost imagine, for even a will of iron to carve its way out.

I told him all this and of his self education, the superhuman work to climb out of his terrible surroundings, and then a marriage made at the age of twenty, simply as a stepping-stone to get his head above water. Then a few years later a tragedy-the death of this wife-a change of place and a renewal of poverty and destitution.

At thirty the forging ahead, domination and ambition telling its tale in the world of men. Then years later, ease, comfort, success--the man a power among his fellows-a factor in whatever city he lived. At forty-five a break, connected- in some way, I said, with that marriage in your early life, " something you did at that moment which crops up again in the hour of your success which will stop your ambition, break your destiny, and I fear also may break your life."

"Stop, for God's sake," he cried, and looking up, my heart bled for the torture his face showed he was undergoing. The hard, cold sceptic who had entered, was now a broken man, the mask was off and big drops of sweat stood like beads on his forehead.

I had not had much pity for him when he entered. I treated him as a surgeon would a patient. I had only thought of proving the truth of this study for which I had slaved for years its success was more to me than anything else. Besides, people did not think of my feelings, for the majority of my callers only paid my fee to expose me as a charlatan if they could get the chance.

But this man, my heart went out in pity to him. I held out my hand.   "Forgive me," I said, "if I have opened up old wounds. Forget what I have told you-perhaps it is all wrong. There are none of us who cannot make mistakes."

"But, my God, it is only too true," he sobbed; "send those people in your waiting-room away, listen to what I must tell you, and help me, for I believe now you can."

I did as he told me, and when we were again alone he began :

"You were right about my early surroundings. I was born in San Francisco, at the age of fifteen I could neither read nor write. My mother was a professional thief, and who my father was I never knew.

"With the desire to learn I used to slip into a mission class on Sunday nights, and from this I got into a night school whenever I got the chance. Finally, a teacher got me into a book store, and I often read half the night through in order to improve my education.

"At twenty I opened a small store of my own, but my want of capital kept me from making headway. About this time I met a woman who pretended she had money, and I married her. Alas ! I soon found I had made a bad bargain.

She had married me for my ambition, believing I would make my way. If I had met a good woman all might have been well, but the woman I had tied myself to was worthless and rapidly gave way to drink, and our life together became one constant quarrel.

"One night, with my disappointed, thwarted ambition rankling in my mind, a worse scene than usual took place, and in a moment of mad passion I killed her. This is the tragedy you saw which ended my marriage. I left the house with the intention of giving myself up to the police, but my ambition got the better of my decision. I could not give in. I determined to rise in life and succeed in spite of my crime. I returned to the house, buried her body in the cellar and baffled all suspicion until my nerves gave way, my business failed, and a year later I left the city.

"Reaching Chicago I took another name, and tried to make a fresh start. In a few years my hard work began to tell. I got into a real estate business. I bought land, and at exactly the age of thirty, I took large offices, and from that time I never looked back. By forty I was a wealthy man, respected by all and considered the most successful man in the city.

"I do not wish to defend myself in any way, but I may say that few men in my city have given more to charity or tried to do more good than I have done.

" I was forty-five a few weeks ago. One morning, while sitting at my office window, I saw a man staring at me through the glass. Suddenly I recognised him, and to my horror I remembered him as the brother of my wife, the woman I had murdered. To get away from the fear of this man I came on here to New York. I came to you, and you tell me that some influence from the tragedy I passed through in my married life will come back again into my fate, break it and probably my life at the very age I have now reached. Do you wonder now at the state of mind I am in?"

I did my best to console him, and as he begged me not to leave him out of sheer pity I passed that evening in his company, and we dined together in his rooms at the Waldorf.

I finally persuaded him to go to Europe. I believed the change and the sea voyage would do him good. He was a rich man, and it did not matter to him where he lived.

The next day I saw him off on the St. Lout's, for Southampton.

Some months passed. I had almost forgotten the incident, when one morning he turned up again in my rooms in Fifth Avenue.

Looking well and in good spirits he told me of his travels, how he liked Europe so much so that he had determined to buy a property near London and pass the remainder of his life abroad.

" But why have you come back? " I asked. "Simply," he said, "to return to Chicago to sell out some property still on my hands. You cannot imagine how a business man hates seeing fools making a mess of his property. In a few weeks I shall be back, and then Europe for the rest of my days."

We had not mentioned the former matter, but I felt a curious misgiving come into my mind as he waved his hand to me that night as the train steamed out of the Great Central Station. Three days later, in a New York paper I read the following:

"STRANGE SHOOTING FATALITY
"Mr.-, a well-known citizen of Chicago, re turned from a trip to Europe on Tuesday evening. On getting off the train and while walking to the handsome house he so recently built, he was shot in the back, and removed in a serious condition to -- Hospital. We regret to learn that there is not any hope entertained of his recovery. The police theory is that Mr.- was struck by a bullet from a shooting-gallery situated not far from where he was found, &c."

A few days later I received the following note, scribbled in pencil.
"-   Hospital, Chicago,
" Thursday.
" DEAR CHEIRO,
"You have doubtless seen the papers. The police theory is of course wrong. I wanted to let you know.   They cannot stop the bleeding, in a few hours all will be over.   Don't put them on the right track. Fate, you see, did play her last card.
" Yours etc."

My readers will understand why I have sup pressed the name of the Hospital and other details. I have also given the name of a city which was not the one he lived in, but in every other respect this story is a verbatim report of what took place.

CHAPTER XVII

A SPIRITUALISTIC SEANCE AND ITS SEQUEL

THE story I am about to relate may sound strange, even impossible, to those who have little experience with the occult, but it is a simple relation of the facts as they occurred, told even in as brief a manner as possible.

One of my clients, a man somewhere about sixty, had waited for close on twenty years to marry the one woman he had ever cared for. I need not enter into details of the difficulties he had to surmount, one alone is sufficient-the woman he loved so passionately was married. A wretched marriage it had been too, but without any possibility of freedom by divorce, for she was a devout Catholic who would not hear of such a thing.

My client was a doctor, a splendid noble hearted man, one of the best men I have ever met, but a man so mentally constituted that he was a rank Materialist, a man who even as a boy had ceased to pray, and on whom not even her influence had had the slightest effect as far as his ideas about a hereafter were concerned.

At last death brought her freedom from her husband, and these two people who loved as I have never seen two people love, were united by marriage at the end of a certain period. Their happiness was, however, short lived; not ten days after the marriage the lady was stricken down with double pneumonia, and in spite of everything science could do she passed away in her husband's arms.

There are no words to describe the state of grief into which this man was plunged; he had no religion to go to for consolation, he had no God to plead with that they might meet again-nothing, nothing, but the most absolute despair.

For weeks I worked with him to give him the courage to live, but on such a mind arguments were useless, life with all it gives had become worse than a torment, the very good he did seemed to mock him, and I was forced to realise that I was fighting worse than a forlorn hope in my efforts to make him live.

One evening we were crossing West 42nd Street on our way to his home. He wanted to give me her picture (I knew well what that meant) and so I walked on ransacking my brain to find some excuse for delay. I don't mind admitting it, no matter what the views of those who read this book may be, but I made every step I took a silent prayer for help that I might save for others the life of a man who did more good in a day than most men do in the whole run of their lives. He was quite cheerful, for as he explained to me he was glad to come to the end of the mockery of existence-so weary that he was happy to think of the rest that he was planning to take.

Suddenly an idea came into my brain. We were passing the rooms of a medium who had on one or two occasions given me remarkable tests of his work. He was not a professional medium just a young man who found he had this peculiar power, and who used it freely for his friends.

I said to the doctor, " Come with me for a moment, we are passing the house of a man who I know is an honest medium, and think how happy you would be if you could get even the slightest message from Anna."

"Alas, my friend," he said, "such happiness is not for me, but I won't argue; if it pleases you I will go with you."

We entered. "Please give us a seance," I asked, "I will tell you later why I want one so badly at this hour."

Mr. X answered, "Gladly, if I can. I may not of course get any results, but I am quite willing to try."

With the brilliant moonlight streaming in through the open windows, we seated our selves round a table in the centre of the room, and in a few moments the medium became entranced.

Then followed a seance I shall never forget. In less than five minutes the doctor was holding a clear and distinct conversation with his wife. At first her voice came very softly-only in whispers, but it was her voice, there was no mistaking that. The medium's face even became like hers, for she had a peculiar droop in the left side of the upper lip and this was the first thing my friend noticed.

Clearly and distinctly she told him that he must not commit suicide, for she said, "You will retard our meeting still more." His life was to be used in work for others, she pleaded, until the moment came when death would release him naturally.

Then she told us a strange bit of philosophy, that she was taken that, through her, he might be led to believe in the reality of the other life that he had always so doubted.

These are only the brief notes of that wonderful seance. I will only add that if Spiritualism never did more it had at least brought peace to one man's heart, and during the ten years he laboured afterwards many hundreds of human beings received the benefit.

CHAPTER XVIII

MARK TWAIN

MARK TWAIN came to see me one afternoon, and the famous humorist was never more serious I think in his life. Up to then I had not seen even his portraits, and I was sorely at a loss "how to place,, the curious rugged piece of humanity that came-to consult me.

As I fell back on my system of working out the dates at which the important happenings take place in the life, my consultant soon began to check off the years I mentioned, and then asked me to explain to him by what method or system I was able to arrive at such conclusions. "The past may leave its mark, I admit," he said, "and character may be told even down to its finest shades of expression; all that I might believe-but how the future may be even foreshadowed, is what I cannot understand."

I reasoned with him that the sub-conscious brain may know in advance what we shall attempt and where we shall fail, that nothing in the world was left to blind chance, and that our very failures were as necessary to our development as were our successes; but seeing I was making no headway towards convincing him I took up the question of heredity as shown by the markings of the hand.

I showed him the impression of a mother's left and right hands with the impression of five of her children's hands, until we came to one when the right hand of the child exactly tallied with the markings on her mother's right hand; in this case, I said, which you can follow up and prove for yourself, every action of this girl's life repeated even to dates the actions of the mother's life, although twenty years separated them in time.

The girl had passed through similar illnesses at the same ages at which they had occurred to the mother; she had married at the same age, had also five children, and was a widow at the same age. Now, I said, if one had known the events of the mother's life and seen that the same markings appeared in the hands of the child then, even say at six years of age, one could have predicted the events which would take place in the fate of the daughter.

This interested my visitor so deeply that he took notes of the various hands I showed him, and we examined with a microscope the lines in the tips of the fingers of the mother and this one daughter, whose fate had been so nearly the same, and we found that even the circles in the finger tips and thumbs also agreed.

As he was going he said, "the one humorous point in the situation is that I came here expecting to lose money by my foolishness, but I have gained a plot for a story on which I shall certainly get back my money." A few years later he published "Pudden Head Wilson," dealing with thumb-marks, which had an enormous success.

Before leaving I asked him to write his name in my autograph book, and he wrote the following, which has made many people laugh since:

"Cheiro has exposed my with humiliating accuracy, confess this accuracy ; still, do it." character to me I ought not to I am moved to

" (Signed) MARK TWAIN "

H. Walter Barnett, 1 Park Side, S.W.

" MARK TWAIN "

CHAPTER XIX

My next important interview was with Ingersoll, the famous atheist, whose lectures and writings are known all the world over.

First, by post, came the impressions of a man's left and right hands, my usual fee, and a typewritten letter requesting the delineation to be sent to a Post Office Box at the City Post Office.

I did the work, but it was not easy-the palm of the hand was large, and out of proportion to the length of the fingers-the sign of the genuine materialist-yet the Line of Mentality was as delicately curved as on the hand of any poet or dreamer of dreams, and so I worked out the picture and sent it off. A week later Ingersoll invited me to call and see him at his house in Fifth Avenue, and to mark his appreciation of what I had written he signed his name to the impression of his right hand, which I have re produced in my book, " Cheiro's Language of the Hand."

MRS. ELLA WHEELER WILCOX

The world knows of Mrs. Ella Wheeler Wilcox through her vivid human poems. It has formed all kinds of opinions of her according to the personal views of her critics. Her famous "Poems of Passion " brought her torrents of abuse, and a whole army of friends. I know of some who would not give this unpretentious little volume room in their houses. I know of others who read and devour each line as they did Bunyan's "Pilgrim's Progress" in their early days.

It may therefore interest both sides if I re count my own experience with this very strongly marked personality. She came, as so many did, without giving any inkling of her name or position. I quickly picked out her wonderful poetic gift, but classed it as of the most dramatic character, at the same time telling her that her versatility of mentality could make of her a brilliant success in any line of literature she would be pleased to make her own. My description of her home life, so sweet and simple, so entirely opposite to what the world might suppose would be the home of the authoress of " Poems of Passion," so impressed her that in her quick impulsive way she said, "You must know my husband, for my life is just as you describe."

Then, at the end of the interview, she told me her name, and I con- fess I was astonished, for I had heard of her fame long before I had left England, and I also had probably formed a wrong conclusion from what I imagined such an authoress would be like.

I have since learned how much public persons are judged wrongly, and as I have later still followed her career, I have become more and more impressed that the soul in its prison-house writes its biography in the lines of the hand with a faithfulness of description that is nowhere else to be found.

This wonderful little woman-for she is wonderful-is so complex that few can make her out, and still fewer can describe her; all are dazzled by her abilities, amazed by her versatility; but beneath all is the deeper human interest that breathes like life itself through every subject she approaches, through every work into which she throws her heart.

I will not attempt to describe her, lest in my attempt I should not do her justice.

The last time we met was in Paris, a little dinner-party at her hotel, only herself, her husband, and Mr. and Mrs. Vance Thompson. She had heard how I had further developed my system of numbers and their occult meaning, and so I had to tell her something at least about this branch of my studies.

I had no need to make a convert; she herself had studied deeply in occult matters of all kinds, and her quick brain grasped my arguments almost before I had time to utter them.

It was late that night, or rather far into the early hours of the morning, before our little party broke up, and Mr. and Mrs. Vance Thompson and myself walked up the Champs Elysees still discussing the wonderful personality of this strangely gifted woman.

MR. GEORGE PERKINS

Among the many who came at this period was Mr. George Perkins, then an unknown quantity, some years later J. P. Morgan's right-hand man, and later still one of the great powers in New York finance.

I remember as if it were yesterday how enthusiastic I got over the future shown in this young man's hands-he was about thirty then, and so quiet and unassuming that one could easily have taken him for a clerk on fifteen dollars a week. He could not believe what I told him of the important career which would so rapidly open before his eyes. He had one of the best head lines I have ever seen, showing a clear mathematical grasp of whatever financial proposition would be laid before his mind, and yet always an unassuming man who would go into the battle prepared for all emergencies, weighing every possibility which could arise, but counting on his own personality last.

Such a man could not lose his head through vanity. I had even the greatest difficulty in persuading him that one half I said could ever come true. But he has written to me since, and so I know he remembers our meeting as well as I do myself.

CHAPTER XX

SOME of my readers may perhaps be dis appointed that I do not relate more about the leaders of American Society, and especially those in the fierce limelight of New York, but my reason for not doing so is the following:

I want this book to be a human document full of human interest, and nothing more.

The American Society papers are always full of descriptions of the doings of New York's "four hundred," as the inner circle there of Society is called, but for my own part I think nothing is more tedious than to keep continually reading of a certain favoured set whose chief asset is that they have more money than any one else, and whose chief aim in life seems to be to give big dinners which, however good, are only useful in upsetting the digestion of so-called friends-or in fact killing them off before their time.

These "pets of society " came to me in their hundreds, but the only two questions which seemed to interest them were, "When shall I have more money?" or, "When shall I be free to marry again?"

I do not suggest for a moment that this set is worse in New York than anywhere else; they are less hypocrites there, that is all; but this same set of people all the world over is much the same-why then should I waste time by discussing them as if they were anywise different in New York from those in other cities of the globe?

Fate does not make her tools of such a class-they are so weighted with money that she passes them by, and going out into " the highways and byways " she selects other material to be the "workers of purpose," the builders of "to be."

For this reason "the society leaders " of any city will not, with very few exceptions, have much part in this chronicle of events. They will be none the worse off-I only hope my readers will be the better for my selection of the "workers" I have chosen.

I shall now relate a story of a man-and a picture-a strange story, which I think I am justified in saying could only have taken place in that Wonderland of Things-the United States.

A tall handsome man called one afternoon a man remarkably frank, who told me he had no money to pay my fee, but who believed "his hands might interest me."

I admit they did; they were hands almost cap able of anything in the field of endeavour, strange hands with the artistic instinct running through them in every direction, and which seemed the whole basis of their being.

I will not weary my reader with description a short resume of the life will be sufficient.

The man had, even in his boyhood, supported his parents by any occupation which came in his way, and by which he could earn an honest penny. An artist at even ten years of age, when he could not afford to buy canvases, he painted pictures on wood.

At twenty he had built for himself a studio, made by his own handiwork in a lonely forest on the edge of the Hudson in New Jersey.

Bit by bit he sold sketches he made, until he could buy a canvas large enough to carry the picture he had one day determined to paint.

And the subject? you ask. Nothing more or less than "The Christ."

This man had had a dream, or a vision, I suppose we should call it, that if he would make the effort The Christ Himself would teach him how to do it.

As he built his own studio, so also he mixed and made his own paints. He had never had a lesson in drawing in his life, he had been too poor to travel to see the world's pictures of Christ, yet his faith was so large that he attempted the great work which he had set him self to do.

No romance of pictures that I have ever heard is greater than what this man endured out in those lonely woods of New Jersey, in order to accomplish his self-imposed task.

Finally it was finished, and on an easel over twenty feet high the head and shoulders of The Christ stood out at the end of the studio on a strange background of purple blue, for all the world like a piece of the sky at night before the stars come out between the day and dark.

For months this man lived looking at what he had created-learning a philosophy of life from those eyes of Christ, and starving to death even while he learned it.

One wild stormy night with the darkness of the woods made blacker by the reflection of the studio lamp, a sharp knock came on the door and was repeated a second and a third time.

For him who had no visitors the occurrence was startling enough, but still more so when he opened the door and two escaped convicts in their terrible striped prison garb pushed past him and quickly fastened the door.

Food l was all they said, and like hungry wolves they seemed ready to spring at his throat.

Food he had none, there was not even a loaf of bread in the place.

It is hard to say what might have happened with such hungry, desperate men, if at that moment one of them had not caught sight of the face of Christ which loomed up like a living thing at the end of the studio.

The next second those men were prostrate before it, and in that silence of death with the moaning of the wind outside, Christ perhaps heard their story-and also their prayer for forgiveness.

Suddenly the tramp of feet surrounded the door and a sharp knock echoed through the place.

When the police entered the artist alone stood before them-all sign of the men had disappeared.

Quickly the officer exclaimed: "Two of the most dangerous criminals escaped from Sing Sing to-night, and seeing the light we thought they might have broken in here-but "-and instinctively looking at the face of Christ with its eyes of pity, he added: "surely this is not the place where convicts will be found. Good night, sir, sorry to have disturbed you; come on, men, we can't waste time here."

When all was quiet two convicts crept out from behind the picture, and kneeling down before the Christ they vowed to forsake their life of crime, and follow as best they could in His footsteps.

These two men are still living-they never turned back-but are doing heroic work to-,day in another country in the cause of Christ.

CHAPTER XXI

THE ATTEMPT ON MY LIFE : SAVED BY A CIGARETTE CASE

THERE are few persons who can go through any form of public life without sooner or later experiencing some danger, and J proved no exception to this rule.

During the summer of I 894 I was hard at work in New York writing my now well-known "Language of the Hand.,, As I was so occupied all day I was forced to do this work in the evenings after dinner, and consequently after six I refused interviews to all callers.

One Saturday evening about 9.30 my secretary came in from the reception room and said, " In spite of every excuse I can make, there is a very gentlemanly-looking man outside who insists on seeing you; he says it is of the greatest importance to him, and he will be very grateful if you will break your rule and give him an interview now."

I said, "Well, perhaps he is in some trouble and I may be able to give him some help or advice-show him in."

I pushed aside the printer's proofs I :was correcting, and went to my consulting table over which there was a very strong electric light.

The man entered : I only noticed a gentlemanly looking person dressed in a frock coat, clean shaven, hair cut close and turning grey at the sides. He had an anxious look on his face, and • nervous manner. On account of the heat of the evening, the door of my consulting room was open. He noticed it and said: "That leads out on the stairs, does it not?"

They were the only words he uttered. As I followed my habit of examining the left hand first, he, finding the right free, slipped it into the breast of his frock coat.

I had not spoken. I was stooping forward looking closely at the lines of the left hand, when, quick as a flash, he slipped his right from its position and made a savage blow straight at my heart with a long pointed dagger.

The force of the blow knocked me off my chair and threw me against the writing table-the dagger had struck a heavy cigarette case in my waistcoat pocket and pierced it. This cigarette case, may add, had only a short time previously been presented to me by Madame Nordica. Without this shield I certainly should not have had a ghost of a chance against such a well aimed blow.

I endeavoured to grasp a small revolver which curiously enough I had persuaded a client the day before to leave in my possession as I was afraid he had suicidal tendencies. Before I could seize it I saw the glint of the dagger flash again in the light of the lamp, and the next second I received a stab that went through my clothes and into my side. He tried to pull the dagger out, but the same moment I grabbed the revolver and fired.

The noise of a revolver was evidently what he dreaded most. With a curse he was out of the door, down the stairs and into Fifth Avenue in less time than it takes me to write. People rushed from the apartments above me, an ambulance call was put in, and then the police arrived on the scene.

As I did not consider I was badly enough injured to be taken to hospital, a doctor was sent for who stitched up the wound and looked after me for the best part of the night.

The incident created a considerable amount of stir; the principal newspapers had long articles about it, and, at all events, it proved by the number of letters which I received that I had made a fast friend of the great American public. The police did their utmost to find the aggressor but without result, and it was some consider able time before I was able to get to the bottom of this mysterious attack.

Over a year later a priest called to see me.   He came, he told me, to talk over the mysterious affair, and finding that I laughed at the whole thing, and bore no enmity against whoever had stabbed me, he then promised that if I would not take any action in the matter he would unveil the mystery.

I gave him my word, and he related the following story :

Some time ago, he said, you had as a client a young woman whose life I must admit you described with remarkable accuracy.

You had told her that her career up to thirty years of age had been ruined by the influence of a man she had come in contact with at the age of eighteen. At the moment of the thirtieth year (you even told her the month) she would at last get an opportunity of breaking from this illegal union, and if she would only take this opportunity, she would be able to start in life again and make a considerable success out of what was up to then a ruined career.

The opportunity occurred, as you had said, and the young woman attempted to take advantage of it, but in an unguarded moment she told this man that she was acting on your advice, and would decide definitely after seeing you again on the following Monday.

Blinded to everything but his own infatuation, this man decided that she should not get the opportunity of consulting you again; so he came on that Saturday evening determined, if possible, to put you out of the way.

Now you have the story, but it is not yet finished-this man lies now at the point of death, he has repented of his act, he has become a good Catholic, but he cannot die in peace until he knows you have forgiven him. I came as his ambassador, I found you bore no ill-will to your assailant, and so I have told you the truth about the matter, which may put your mind at rest about any fear you might have had of a second attack.

Half an hour later the good father and myself stood at this man's bedside; he heard from my own lips that I forgave him fully and freely, and I had the satisfaction of knowing that on this point at all events he died in peace.

The bright spot in this history is that the woman in question had even by then got on the road toward success, and shortly afterwards married one of the wealthiest men in New York. One night, years later, she saw me dining in a celebrated restaurant in Paris, and as she left with her husband she stopped at the door, and calling waiter, sent me the following pencilled message, which, in her characteristic handwriting, is lying before me as I write.

"I owe my life's success and happiness to you-may God bless you for it."

"CHEIRO" EXPERIMENTING WITH PROFESSOR DODIARDI'S "THOUGHT MACHINE"

CHAPTER XXII

I WILL pass over many incidents which marked my first visit to New York and go on to my return to London at the fall of I 896.

Within a week of my arrival in my rooms in Bond Street I had the same rush of visitors as before.

On this occasion I exhibited for the first time a very curious machine which for want of a better name I called a "Register of Cerebral Force," which· had been invented by my old friend, Professor Savary d'Odiardi. Professor d'Odiardi, as many others can testify, was one of the most remarkable men that perhaps ever lived, in his experiments on the hidden forces of the body and perhaps also of the spirit.

He was a descendant of the famous family of the Duke de Revigo, one of the First Napoleon's great generals. He had the right to use the famous old name and title but he preferred his more simple family name of Savary d'Odiardi.

He was endowed with so many talents that in the embarras de richesses he never knew exactly which to use for the best, and he certainly never seemed to use any for his own personal advantage.

He had had a sensational career. At the age of fifteen the gold medal of the Academy of Music, Paris, was divided between himself and Gounod. Perhaps it was the division of this great prize that hurt his pride, for in the end he did not follow music, except for his own pleasure.

There are many persons living in London to-day who will bear me out if I say that one never realised the power of music until one had heard this old man with the monk's head play the organ, piano or harp as he did at times in his own house in Cromwell Road, Kensington. On these occasions it was often the human harp he swept his fingers over, for I have seen men and women, and some of them the most iron-bound specimens that could be imagined, break down as he told their story in music, and steal up to his side and confess the sealed pages of their life's history.

He had also studied medicine and had held a distinguished post under the Government of Napoleon the Third. Law he had also mastered, and had fought and won an important case before the French Courts and restored to a woman her husband who had been falsely condemned some years before.

Such is a very brief description of this remark able man who for years had been one of my best friends in London, and from whom also

Chart for d'Odiardi's Thought-Photography and Register of Cerebral Force.

See Dr. Bcradue's report and letters to Academy of Sciences, Paris.

REGISTERED AT STATIONERS' HALL.

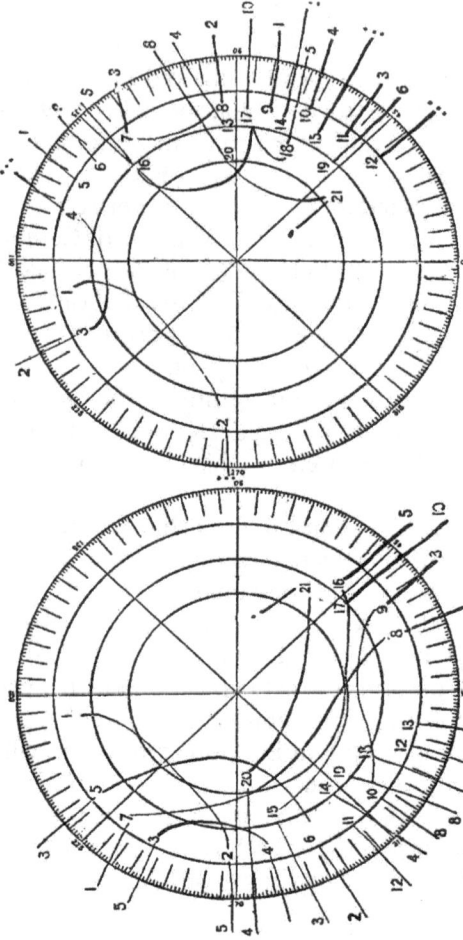

No. 1   MR. LIONEL PHILLIPS, FEB. 17TH, 1897.

REV. RUSSELL WAKEFIELD, FEB. 27TH, 1897.   No. 2

Explanation of Movement.

The needle started at 1, went to 2, from 2 to 3, from 3 to 4, and so on with the numbers marked inside the chart.

The numbers outside show the duration of the stoppage, viz: In No. 1 chart it will be ▬ that at No. 2 movement the needle remained for five seconds before it moved to 3, whereas in No. 2 chart at No. 2 movement it would not remain steady.

I learned a great deal of occult knowledge. Rumour said that he had in the many vicissitudes of his career been a member of the Trappist Order, but rumour utters so many lies about men who are in any way above the ordinary that I never gave much credence to this, except on certain occasions, when I knew he was in close communication with the Vatican and the late Pope. Once when I visited Rome he gave me letters of introduction which opened to me the most inaccessible doors in the Eternal City.

Still, we never discussed religion except from the occult standpoint, which was the one common ground that had brought us together.

Speaking of my visit to Rome reminds me of a curious incident which may be of interest to my readers.

It had been my custom every afternoon to wander into St. Peter's and sit for an hour or so in the half-shadow of one of the chancels.

I cannot explain why I did this, except perhaps that it was the " calling" of that devotional temperament which I have already alluded to in previous chapters.

On one of these occasions I noticed that I was apparently an object of interest to a strange old man who had followed me through the chapel.

He was a man so old and worn by Time that it was impossible even to guess at his age. His wonderful, intelligent face looked like a mask of polished marble, while his long white beard and white hair seemed in strange contradiction to his black eyes, that had all the appearance of youth and vigour.

Although nearly bent double by age, there was yet something so impressive about his appearance that it attracted attention and almost reverence.

Seeing me looking at him he came towards me, and speaking softly in French said:

"Will you please meet me here to-morrow evening at five o'clock? There is something I want to give you which may be of help to you later in life."

Almost before I had said, "Yes," he turned and walked slowly down the nave and out into the street.

The next day I was at the agreed rendezvous even before the hour he had appointed.

I had not long to wait. I soon saw him approaching from the shadow of one of the small side-chapels, and as he crossed the chancel I realised then how very old he must have been.

Taking me by the arm he led me to a stone seat under one of the windows, and handing me a large packet tied up in an old leather covering he said: "My young friend, I have watched you coming here for a long time; but it is not religion that draws you here, for you are, as I am, a seeker after the great truth that needs no chapel of stone for its sanctuary."

"What do you mean?" I asked.

THE HERO OF THE SPANISH-AMERICAN WAR
Autographed photo given to me by Admiral Dewey on his return after
the destruction of the Spanish Fleet

"I mean," he replied, "and I know I make no mistake, that you are even as I have been-a seeker after occult things, an initiate in that great religion that gets its light from the stars and its faith from symbols and signs that contain the mystery of life for all those who seek its meaning in the right way.

"I have come to the end of my appointed time, but you have yet a long course of years before you. I want you then to take this manuscript and study it with those occult studies that I know by your face, and from another system of reading, you are absorbed in nearly as much perhaps as I have been myself.

"The greater part of this manuscript has been carefully copied from the most ancient Egyptian works on occultism which have been lost in the burning of the Library of Alexandria. You will find what I am giving you will be of great value later in your life ; as for myself, I am happy to have found in you a person who will use these studies, and who will keep the lamp of this sacred knowledge burning brightly even in this age of materialism."

Almost before I could thank him, the old man had said adieu and disappeared through a side door into the street.

Dumbfounded with amazement, I returned to my hotel and found, to my astonishment, that I had in my possession a carefully written manuscript containing extracts on many studies of occultism, the originals of which were, as is well known, lost in the Library of Alexandria just as this strange old man had told me.

But to return to my friend in London and the curious machine which he had invented.

When quite a young man, as Edouard Savary d'Odiardi, he had presented the first of these "Thought Recorders" to the Academy of Sciences in Paris and it was investigated there and considered very wonderful.

In this first machine the needle could be willed by a person to move about thirty degrees, but in the one which he afterwards perfected a person, without touching it and standing even at a distance of three feet away, could make the needle move to about 160 degrees of a circle, and more wonderful still could by an effort of his will make the needle stand steady at certain points on its return journey.

This instrument certainly attracted considerable attention, All kinds of people came to be tested by it-so much so that I often sent my friend cheques to the amount of £ 20 per week as royalty for my using it. People who took drugs, especially morphine, or who were weak minded, could hardly make the needle move, and had little or no power over it, while with habitual drunkards it moved in a peculiar jerky manner that was unmistakable.

So much as a prelude to the experiment I am about to relate. One day a man with a very strong will stood before the instrument and at the distance of three feet forced the needle to mark a very high point on the disc. At this point he was holding the needle steady, which was a very remarkable thing to do, when some one came into the room and mentioned to a friend that a certain share that was being- actively dealt with

Chart for d'Odiardi Thought-Photography and Register of Cerebral Force, on the Stock Exchange had broken half an hour before and had already fallen considerably.

No one in the room knew that the man standing at the machine was interested in the particular stock in question, but the moment the news was announced he lost all power over the needle, and, in spite of every effort he could make, it retreated back to its starting-point.

Only then it was that the man before the instrument turned and confessed to the mental shock the news had given him.

On the previous page will be found illustrations of two experiments, one with Mr. Lionel Phillips and the other with the Reverend Russell Wake field, which are interesting as showing how the needle in one case worked altogether to the left and in the other case to the right side of the dial.

Among the many well-known people with whom I experimented with this curious machine was Gladstone himself. He was profoundly interested in it, but I shall relate my interview with him later on in its proper place.

CHAPTER XXIII

ABOUT this time I was introduced to Mrs. H. M. Stanley (later Lady Stanley, the wife of the famous African explorer), and I was invited to meet Stanley himself at luncheon in their house in Richmond Terrace.

I must say I rather dreaded this interview, for I had heard a good deal of Stanley's brusque manner with people in whom he took no interest, and I rather imagined that we should have no interest in common.

I was, however, completely mistaken; it is true that all the way through the luncheon he never opened his lips, but when the ladies had retired, and we were left alone, to my astonishment he put out his hands for me to read, and in a few moments we were talking as if we had been old friends.

He went back over the past, reviewed it step by step, explained to me how he had been misjudged by those who had not perhaps weighed the circumstances under which he was placed. I heard from his own lips of that memorable tramp across darkest Africa. He seemed to live every moment as he spoke of the anxieties and responsibilities he had to meet, but not one word did he say of his own personal dangers.

It was a memorable afternoon for me, but I am glad to say it was not the only time I had the honour of meeting the man I must always remember as "the great Stanley."

At a subsequent visit to Richmond Terrace, to my astonishment, he suggested that I should meet Gladstone. "Mrs. Stanley will arrange it for you, if you like," he said. Mrs. Stanley agreed, and sat down at once and wrote the letter.

By return of post came one of Gladstone's famous postcards offering me an appointment for the following day at Hawarden Castle. That night I took the train to Chester, and the next day at three o'clock kept my appointment.

AUTOGRAPHED PHOTOGRAPH GIVEN TO ME BY
MR. GLADSTONE, AUGUST 3, 1897

CHAPTER XXIV

THE MEETING WITH W. E. GLADSTONE

IT was a hot day in August. Mr. Gladstone had the day before made what was, I believe, his last public speech, when he addressed the Horticultural Society of Chester.

Mrs. Gladstone met me in the hall, and my heart sank as she said that Mr. Gladstone was so fatigued that she must refuse to have him disturbed on any pretext.

I told her how sorry I was to hear of Mr. Gladstone's indisposition, but that I should only be too happy to come up again from London any time he wished, and I turned to go. •

At this moment the "grand old man" opened the door of his study and said: "My dear, is that the gentleman who has an appointment with me at three o'clock?"

Mrs. Gladstone replied, "Yes, but you must not see any one to-day."

"But, my dear," he replied, " this man has come all the way from London at my invitation. He is a friend of the Stanleys, and it will interest me to see him."

"Sir," I said, " please do not consider me. I will come up from London another day when you are feeling better."

"I will see you now," he answered, and then, with a sad tone in his voice, he added, "I may never be better than I am to-day."

We walked into his well-known study. He motioned me to a seat by the window. One of my own books lay on a table by his side, and I saw to my surprise that he had evidently deter mined to know something about my study before he met me. (This I have since heard was his invariable custom, the reading up before hand of any subject on which he was about to be interviewed.)

But there was a still greater surprise in store, and also an example of his wonderful memory. " I have been told that you are the son of So-and So," he said, "your father had the same love of higher mathematics that I have. We have corresponded many times on difficult problems here is one which he worked out about twelve years ago, and which has interested me many times since," and as he spoke he unrolled several sheets of paper covered with calculations and an algebraical figure in my father's handwriting.

"Is your father still living? " he asked.

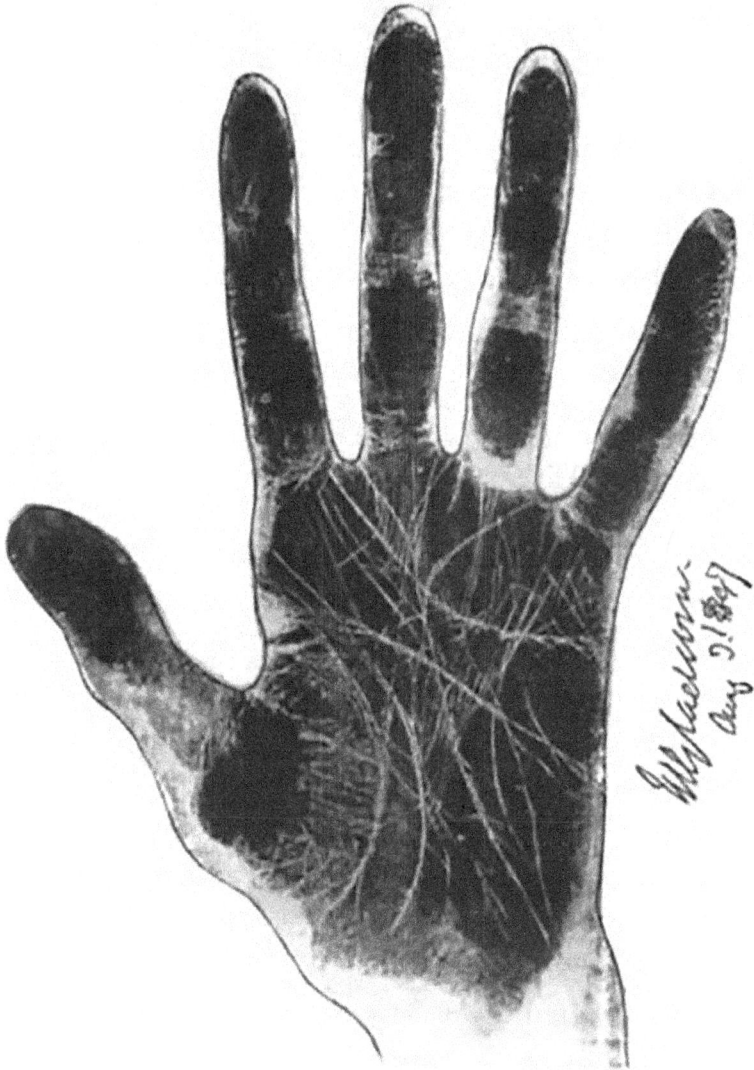

THE RIGHT HAND OF GLADSTONE, TAKEN
AUGUST 3, 1897

"No, sir," I answered, "he passed away only a short time ago."

"And you," he said, "have you inherited the same love of figures and mathematics ? "

"Alas, no," I replied, "my calculations only relate to occult things, and they probably will not interest you."

"We will see later," he said; "now please let me hear your theories about this subject that the Stanleys tell me you are a master -of. Speak slowly and clearly so that I may follow you if I can."

The gentleness and kindness of this wonderful man-this man who had so often swayed the destinies of nations-whose intelligence was acknowledged even by his enemies, completely conquered my nervousness, and, astonished at my own confidence, I plunged at once into my subject. At first I rapidly explained the theories associated with the study, and backed them up with the impressions of hands showing heredity and other signs, and then attempted to show, that man, like everything else in life, has his number as well as his place in this universe, and that, if this number could be determined, so could the years that corresponded to this number be equally determined either for his good or evil as the case might be.

Taking as an illustration the different vibrations in each tone of music, with a very simple instrument I had with me I showed him how each vibration produced different forms in matter, and that the same vibration repeated dozens and hundreds of times always created a distinct figure of its own that never varied in its basic principles, that these tones or vibrations had their distinct number, and so on through the scale of creation up to man, who as the image of the universe vibrated in exact accordance with the vibrations of those planets which, as the instruments of God, called the universe itself into being.

I had brought with me my friend Savary d'Odiardi's machine, which I have described in a previous chapter, and placing it on the study table I asked Mr. Gladstone to test for himself if every person brought before it did not affect it in a distinctly different manner according to their willpower radiating outward through the atmosphere.

Standing near the instrument I showed him how far I was able to will the needle to turn; he then tried it himself, and calling some of the servants into the room he quietly tested it with one after another.

When we were again alone I asked him to allow me to take a chart of the movements of the needle when operated on by his will, and I may add that of the thousands of examples I have made with this instrument Mr. Gladstone's stands out as the most remarkable for will force and concentration, as shown by the length of time he was able to make the needle remain at certain points.

Before the end of the interview he allowed me to take impressions of his hands for my collection, and further to show his interest he auto graphed and gave me the photograph of himself which I reproduce here.

The date on it is Aug. 3, 1897.

Mrs. Gladstone finally broke the interview by coming in and announcing that it was half-past six. I felt rather guilty, but as if to save me from her anger he said, "My dear, this has been one of the most interesting afternoons I think I have ever spent; I am not fatigued, I am now going to show this young man the gardens, for it is he who must be tired."

Together we walked out over that lawn so beautifully kept that it looked like a matchless piece of green velvet set with those gorgeous crimson geraniums which he loved so much. He made me talk of America, and he said how much he regretted that he had never seen that great country and spoke of the deep interest he took in the progress the United States had made during those long years over which his memory stretched.

Finally he said good-bye, and as I reached the gate I stood for a moment and watched his retreating figure pass on through the gardens and disappear among the red and the green _and the dying glory of the sun.

CHAPTER XXV

A STRANGE EXPERIENCE AND ITS SEQUEL

ONE morning I received the following letter, written on cheap paper, in scratchy, bad handwriting:
"WALTHAM CROSS,
"August 19, 1897.
" DEAR Srn,-What would you charge to come down to this place, about twenty miles from London, and read the hand of a child unable to go to town? Please reply to X, care of post office, Waltham Cross.
" Respectfully yours,
"X."

My first thought was, "People of this class would never pay my fee/' but to my surprise, in answer to my secretary's letter, there came another scratchy note, accepting my offer, and arranging the following Sunday for my visit.

Sunday came, a hot summer like day. I caught my train at Broad Street and started to solve what even then I thought a mystery.

The letter had evidently been written by an elderly woman, and I could not quite reconcile the idea of people, uneducated and probably poor, paying such a price to have a child's hand read, even if it was an invalid, and unable to come to town. They were also suspicious, for they had not given name or address. My sole directions were to get out at Waltham Cross, and under the clock in the waiting room, I would find a man ready to lead me to my destination.

Alighting at Waltham Cross, I followed the directions and found a man anxiously looking out for some one to arrive. Step ping up to him, I said: "My name is 'Cheiro.' You are looking for me, are you not?"

Looking me over from head to foot he slowly answered, " Yes, I've been waiting for you waiting some time, too."

Leaving the station, we turned toward the town. I naturally asked how far we had to walk, and received the vague reply that we would go a short way by the fields, and with out any more explanation he turned down a path that led across the country at almost right angles to the town. A walk of ten minutes brought us again to the road, and crossing it we entered one of those old-fashioned private lanes that are to be found in so many parts of England.

We came at last to the beautiful country seat of Sir Henry and Lady

Elliott & Fry, London

SIR H. M. STANLEY.

Meux, and I insisted on stopping to admire the old arch of Temple Bar which had been carted down from the very heart of busy London, and placed as an entrance gate in the quiet and calm of the country. I thought if those stones could speak what tales they could tell of the hundreds of fortunates and unfortunates who had entered that old gateway of the city ! I made some remark of this kind to my companion, and he gruffly replied that he " didn't . think much of them sentimental ideas," that he didn't believe in God, man or devil, and, furthermore, he added: "I don't believe in you, anyhow. It's one of them sentimental ideas that made my old woman send for you to come down here and tell her how long a certain party's got to live."

Ah, I thought, so that's what she wants to know. Well, I wonder what use such information will be. " Who is the party," I asked, " a relation ? " But the old chap evidently repented having said so much, and I could not get him to utter another word until ten minutes later we turned off the path and entered a long straggling wood that seemed to have no end. At last, when I was be ginning to grumble at the length of my walk, my companion turned toward an old house, little better than a hut, on the outskirts of the wood, and in a few moments I was respectfully greeted by a sharp-eyed elderly woman who came to the door. In this strange pair, man and wife, I at once recognised one of those extraordinary contrasts so often found among the lower classes. The man, coarse and uneducated, utterly without conscience or principle, associated with a woman also uneducated, yet with an innate niceness of manner that lent a certain grace and refinement to every word, to every action. A woman wily as a snake, unscrupulous in all her dealings, and yet one guided, governed, enslaved by the superstitious fears that held her. She looked upon me as a being possessed by a supernatural power, she would not question whether of God or devil. She wanted that power used for her advantage. That was all she knew or cared.

Leading me upstairs, she opened the door of what was nothing better than an attic. Lying on the floor in the sunlight lay a little girl dressed in rags playing with the long hair that fell around her shoulders. Fixing her large frightened eyes on the woman, she crept away on all fours, and crouched like a dog under a table that occupied a corner of the room.

"Poor little thing, she is frightened," I said. " Oh, she is always that way," the woman replied. " She is a great affliction to me, I can assure you, sir. She is so unlike other children that I can't let her out of the house. She's very delicate, too, and I've often thought, sir, that it would be better if God in His mercy took her away from this world of misery." " Oh, nonsense," I replied. " You should not say that. What's the little one's age ? " After a slight hesitation, she said she did not quite recollect, but that about fourteen would be near it.

"Well," I said, "are these the hands you want me to look at ? "

" Yes, sir," she answered, " and what you will please pay special attention to is, if it be likely that she will live any length of time."

After some coaxing on my part, and a few menaces on the side of the woman, I succeeded in getting the little one to let me see her hands. I was not long in drawing the conclusion that she could not possibly be the child of such parents Hereditary laws influence the hand too much for me to have made any mistake. As the racehorse could not be the foal of the Clydes dale, so it was not possible that this child could be the off-spring of such people. However, I kept my thoughts to myself, but taking a still deeper interest in the hands, I noticed that although the child was evidently born of clever, intellectual people, yet her Line of Mentality showed an utter want of development.

Looking up at the woman, I said sharply : "Is it possible that you have kept the child all these years without education of any kind?" The expression of fear on the woman's face told me the power I had already gained over her, and which I determined to use later for the benefit of the child.

After making half a dozen contradictory excuses, she at last admitted that the child had had no training of any kind, and further more, was so seldom spoken to that she hardly knew any expressions of speech.

"My God," I thought, "is it possible ? " But I soon proved that such was indeed the case. The girl hardly knew even the simplest words in the English language. She could but articulate sounds almost similar to those of animals. A peculiar cry seemed to be her favourite expression, but words she had scarcely any. I was too horrified to read more. Putting down the little hands, I quietly but firmly demanded of the woman the full history of the child. Seized with superstitious fear, her face white as death, she closed the door to prevent the man from hearing, and with the poor little fair-haired mite playing near her feet, she-for probably the first time in her life-told the truth.

The story was to the effect that in her early days she had kept a baby farm in the south west district of London. She had been twice imprisoned for the suspicious deaths of infants in her care, and at last, when about to give up the business, she received an offer from a woman to take charge of a child. A fair annual sum was promised, if she would guarantee that the baby would be taken to some place away from London.

The woman consented, and for fourteen years had lived in that little hut in company with the man I saw, one of the most notorious poachers in the country. She had never had any children of her own, and she had no sympathy with children. The poacher also detested the sight of one. Consequently 1 the poor little mite at our feet had lived almost the whole of its life in that garret. It was cared for and treated almost as one would treat an animal. The only language the child had learned ere the cries of fear : the only knowledge she received was the light and darkness of the day and night.

But why had I been sent for ? Simply because of a strange dream that the woman had, combined with her natural superstition. The money for the little one's support had ceased for two years. Grudging her even the food she used the man had at last determined to kill the child, and bury its body in the wood. The woman, with all the crimes she had committed, for some reason would not consent. She explained that there was some thing uncanny about the child; that she dared not allow it to be killed; that she had an idea that the little thing could not live long, and that finally, having made some money during the past week (I suspect through some robbery in the neighbourhood), she had deter mined to send for me.

Such was the story, and I had good reason to believe it true. I felt that I had been sent there to get that child from their clutches. The woman would be quite willing that I should take the little one away, but the man, I felt sure, would see it dead before letting it go without the payment of the money that was due. If I went to the police, I might spoil all. Besides, I had promised the woman I would not do so. While hesitating what to do or say, I felt I had been brought there to save that poor little scrap of humanity, and so I promised the woman that if she would keep the child safe for a week longer all money due would be paid and a reward as well given to her for resisting the man's murderous plan.

I found my way back to the station troubled and perplexed. I thought if I could only trace the mother of the child I should be certain to touch her heart with my story, but I had not the faintest clue to follow. The woman had been unable to give me any in formation. She had merely received the child from a nurse, and through her had received her monthly payments ; but alas, this woman had disappeared in the last two years. Afraid to trust to my instinct, which told me that I should be able to carry out my promise to save the child, I found myself growing more and more anxious as day after day passed, and I got no nearer the solution of my difficulty.

At last I determined to try some of those good-hearted women who support large in situations for children and foundlings, but I must con fess I found the truth of my story generally doubted, and at last the end of the week arrived without any good having been done. Friday evening came, and with the tragedy of this child ever before me I was studying the hand of one of my consultants, when I noticed what I felt certain I had seen on some hand before-a peculiar knotted blue vein that stood out clear and distinct at the base of the little finger. I tried to re collect where I had seen it, but it seemed as if I could not remember.   Atlast, when I had finished, I asked if there was any question relating to her life that she would like to ask. " Yes," she said, " there is one, and to me it is the most important of all."

I looked up surprised. She was a woman a little over thirty, dressed in widow's weeds-a handsome woman in the very prime of life. " Yes," she went on, " you were right when you said that I had a child when seventeen. I was not married then, and my child was taken away from me in order to save my name. A year later a marriage was arranged by my family to a man I barely knew, and with him I went to live in South Africa. After the death of my husband I have now returned to England, and after fourteen years have learned that the child I was led to believe had died, is still alive, and up to two years ago, was supported by money sent by my father. About this time he died suddenly of heart disease, and now I can get no clue or trace of my little one. Look at my hand again, and for God's sake tell me if I may still have hope."

Like a flash of light, I remembered that knotted blue vein was also in the hand of the child. Such things run in families for generations. The story tallied with what I knew. Why say more? At the last moment I had found the mother of the poor little waif.

CHAPTER XXVI

A BOOK WRITTEN ON HUMAN SKIN

THE success I made in this work was chiefly owing to the fact that, though my principal study was the lines and formation of hands, yet I did not confine myself alone to that particular page in the book of nature, but endeavoured to study every phase of thought that can throw light on human life; consequently the very ridges of the skin, the hair found on the hands, all were used as a detective would use a clue to accumulate evidence. I found people were only sceptical of such a study because they had not had the subject presented to them in a logical or reasonable manner.

There are hundreds of facts connected with the hand that people have rarely if ever heard of, and I think it will not be out of place if I touch on them here.

For instance, in regard to what is known as the corpuscles. Meissner, in 1853, proved that these little molecular substances were distributed in a peculiar manner in the hand. He found that in the tips of the fingers, they were 108 to the square inch, with 400 papillre; that they gave forth certain dis tinct crepitations, or vibrations, and that in the red lines of the hand they were most numerous, and, strange to say, were found in straight individual rows in the lines of the palm.

Experiments were made as to these vibrations, and it was proved that after a little study one could distinctly detect and recognise the crepitations in relation to each individual, that they increased or decreased in every phase of health, thought, or excitement, and were extinct the moment death had mastered its victim.

About twenty years later, experiments were made with a man in Paris, who had an abnormally acute sense of sound (Nature's compensation for want of sight, as he had been born blind). In a very short time by continual practice this man could detect the slightest change or irregularity in these crepitations, and through these changes was able to tell with wonderful accuracy about how old a person was, and how near illness, or even death he might be. The study of these corpuscles was also taken up by Sir Charles Bell, who in 1874 demonstrated that each corpuscle contained the end of a nerve fibre, and was in immediate connection with the brain.

This great specialist also demonstrated that every portion of the brain was in touch with the nerves of the hand and more particularly with those corpuscles which are found in the tips of the fingers and the lines of the hand.

The detection of criminals by taking impressions of the tips of the fingers and by thumb marks is now used, I believe, by the police of almost all countries, and thousands of criminals have been tracked down and identified by this means.

To-day at Scotland Yard one may see almost an entire library devoted to books on this side of the subject and to the collections that the police have made, and yet in my short time I remember how this idea was scoffed at when Monsieur Bertillon and the French police first commenced the detection of criminals by this method. If the ignorant prejudice against a complete study of the hand were overcome, the police would be still more aided by studying the lines of the palm and by a knowledge of what these lines mean, especially as regards mentality and the inclination of the brain in one direction or another.

[4]It is a well-known fact that, even if the skin is burnt off the hands, or removed by an acid, in a short time the lines will reappear exactly as they were before, as do the ridges or" spirals " in the skin of the inside tips of the fingers and thumb.

The scientific use of such a study could also be made 'invaluable in foreseeing tendencies towards insanity, &c.

But prejudice, as all know, is a hard thing to combat, and therefore it is that a study which could render untold aid to humanity has been neglected and despised.

And yet it cannot be denied that this strange study was practised and followed by some of the greatest teachers and students of other

4 In connection with the terrible Houndsditch murders in 1911, the Chief Inspector of Police in replying to the magistrate said he took impressions of the prisoner's finger prints at the court. The hands were not washed or prepared in any way. The following is a reprint from the Daily Telegraph of Feb. 25, 1911.

What is your authority for the proposition that the prints of two different fingers are never alike ?-I say I have never found it so. I am only giving you my own experience.

I want to know what steps you have taken to come to that conclusion ?-I may be able to help you in this way. We have 170,000 sets of prints recorded in the office. During the last ten years, since the introduction of the system, we have made 62,000 identifications-recognitions and, so far as is known, without error. I think that will convey to your mind that we deal in pretty large numbers, and I am justified in telling you that we have never found two impressions taken from different fingers to agree with each other.

civilisations

Whether these ancient philosophers were more enlightened than we are has long been a question of dispute, but the one point, and the most important one which has been admitted, is that in those days the greatest study of mankind was man. It is therefore reasonable to suppose that their conclusions that such subjects were worthy of the deepest attention and respect are more likely to be correct than those of an age like our own, famous chiefly for its implements of destruction, its warships, its dynamite and its cannon.

This study of hands can be traced back to the very earliest period of civilisation and also to the most enlightened. It has been practised by the greatest minds in all those civilisations that have left their mental philosophies and their monuments for us to marvel at. India, China, Persia, Egypt, Rome, all have set the greatest store on this study of the hand.

During my stay in India I was permitted by some Brahmins, descendants of the Joshi caste, famous from time immemorial for their· knowledge in occult subjects, with whom it was my good fortune to become intimately acquainted, to make extracts on such subjects from an extraordinary book that they regarded as almost sacred, and which belonged to the great past of the now despised Hindustan.

This strange book was made of human skin, pieced and put together in the most ingenious manner. It was of an enormous size, and contained hundreds of well-drawn illustrations, and records of how, when, and where this or that mark was proved correct. One of the most extraordinary features in connection with it was that it was written with some red liquid which age had no power to spoil or destroy. I need hardly add that the effect of those vivid red letters on the pages of dull yellow skin was most remarkable and most uncanny. By some compound-one probably made of herbs-each page was glazed, as it were, by varnish, but whatever this compound was, it seemed to defy time, as the outer cover alone show d signs of wear and decay. As regards its enormous age, there could be no question. It had been written in three sections or divisions, representing three distinct portions of time. The first part belonged to the earliest Aryan language, and dated so far back that very few even of the Brahmins themselves could read or decipher this portion of its pages.

As the wisdom of this strange race spread far and wide across the earth, so the theories and ideas about this study spread and were practised in other countries. In the same way in which religion suits itself to the conditions of the country in which it is propagated, so this lore divided itself into systems, but it is to the days of the Grecian Civilisation that we owe the present clear and lucid form of the study.

The Greek Civilisation has in many ways been considered the highest and most intellectual in the world, and here it is that Cheiromancy (from the Greek, Cheir, the hand) grew and found favour in the eyes of those who have given us laws and philosophies that . we employ to-day.

We find that the philosopher Anaxagoras taught and practised it about the year 423-B.c. We also find that Hispanus discovered, on an altar dedicated to Hermes, a book on Cheiromancy, written in gold letters, which he sent as a present to Alexander the Great, as "a study worthy the attention of an elevated- and inquiring mind." Instead of being followed by the "weak-minded" we find, on the contrary, that it numbered amongst its disciples such men of learning as Aristotle, Pliny, Paracelsus, Cardanus, Albertus Magnus, the Emperor Augustus and many others of note.

This brings us down to the period when the power of the Church was beginning to be felt outside the domain and jurisdiction of religion. It is said that the early Fathers were jealous of the power of this old-world science. Whether this is true or not, we find that it was bitterly denounced and persecuted by the early Church. Alas I it has always happened that the history of any dominant creed or sect is the history of opposition to knowledge unless that know ledge come through it.

This study, therefore, the offspring of "pagans and heathens," was not even given a trial. It was denounced as sorcery and witchcraft ; the devil was conjured up as the father of all such students, and the result was that in those days people were more afraid of owning such a parentage than they are now, and through this bitter persecution this study was outlawed and fell into the hands of vagrants, tramps and gypsies. In spite of this persecution it is interesting and significant to note that almost the first book ever printed was a work on Palmistry, "Die Kunst Ciromantia,11 printed in Augsburg, in the year 1475.

In examining this subject we shall find that, as in the study of mankind it came to be recognised that there was a natural position on the face for the nose, eyes, lips, &c., so also on the hand it was seen that there was a natural position for what became known as the Line of Head, Line of Life and so on, and that if these were found in unnatural positions they would equally be the indications of unnatural tendencies. (See plates" The Hand of a Murderer," pg. 72, and" The Hand of a Suicide," pg. .111.) It doubtless took years of study to name these lines and marks, but then, as I stated before, it must be remembered that this curious study is more ancient than any other in the world.

The original Hebrew of the Book of Job, chap. xxxvii. and verse 7, may be rendered in these significant words : " God caused signs or seals on the hands of all the sons of Men, that the sons of men might know their works."

As the student of anatomy can build up the entire system from the examination of a single bone, so may a person by a careful study of an important member of the body such as the hand, apart from anything superstitious-or even mystical-build up the entire action of the system and trace every effect back to its cause.

To-day the science of the present is coming to the rescue of the so-called superstition of the past. All over the world scientists are little by little sweeping aside prejudice and beginning to study so-called occult questions, and perhaps the " whys " and " wherefores" of such things may one of these days be as clearly explained as are those wireless waves of electricity that to-day carry our messages from land to land.

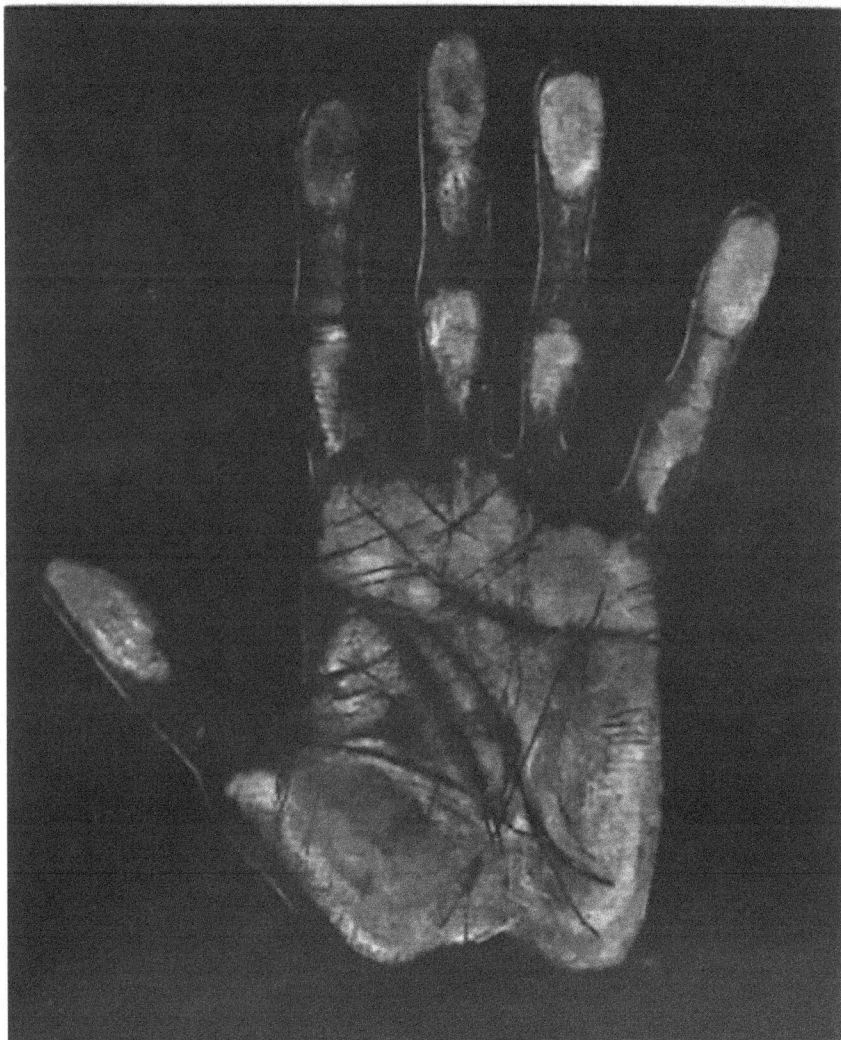

THE HAND OF A SUICIDE

Compare this hand with that of Dr. Meyer, shown earlier in this book, for the abnormal position of the line of mentality

Stereoscopic Company, Regent St., W.

PROFESSOR MAX MÜLLER

CHAPTER XXVII

PROFESSOR MAX MULLER

LUNCHING one Sunday with Colonel and Mrs. Kingscote in their country home in Oxford, I was surprised to see Professor Max Muller coming across the lawn with my large book, "The Language of the Hand," with its black and white cover under his arm.

I was astonished to hear that such a man found my book of sufficient interest to come and ask me questions on the subject, and even still more so when he showed me the pencilled marks he had made in the margin of certain chapters.

After tea he insisted on my going back with him to his library, and there, amid his many Sanskrit treasures, for the next two hours he translated for me passages he thought would prove useful to me for further works on the subject.

Alas, I can never describe the simplicity of this great man, the acknowledged most eminent Sanskrit scholar in the world, or his kindness towards me. I indeed learned that day that it is only the great who can afford to be simple.

Many of the volumes in his wonderful library dealt with the occult mystery of numbers, and he seemed particularly interested in the practical way in which I had evolved my system so as to make numbers a key to many things that concern life, thought and time. When at the end of several hours' conversation I rose to go, as I told him how deeply I appreciated his condescension, in the kindest way possible to imagine he said: "My dear sir, you forget you are just as great in your special study as I am perhaps in mine. We are fellow students all, even if some of us have Professor's chairs while others have not even stools to sit upon."

A week later he called on me in London to give me an impression of his hand for my collection, and from then until I left in the following year for a return visit to the States he paid me periodical visits, and on nearly every occasion he brought with him some old book or some translation which he thought would benefit me in my work.

Now as I look back over the years that have passed I appreciate more than ever such moments, and am lost in amazement that Fate so favoured me.

And yet I see now that these favours encouraged me to work all the harder. I almost treated the study that gave me so much as one would some sacred path that made the rough places of life smooth, and so it was that the more I received the more I gave-magnetism, mentality, every thing I had to give-to the tired men and women of the world who came to listen to the message of life which it was my privilege to translate to them.

LORD RUSSELL OF KILLOWEN
Late Lord Chief Justice of England

CHAPTER XXVIII

IN preceding chapters I have explained that by finding the key to the number which seems to govern a person's life I was able with considerable accuracy to foresee what year, and, in some cases, in what month the climax of the life's career would be attained. The following is a peculiar instance of this.

One day in the middle of one of my seasons in London a very exacting and apparently severe old gentleman came to see me. There was certainly nothing in his appearance or dress to lead me for a moment to imagine that he was even then a very big man in his profession.

Dates, however, seemed to interest him, and when I told him certain years in his past life which had caused important changes in his career, he did me the honour to delve back into his memory of the past and give me the satisfaction of knowing that the years I gave him were correct. I then told him that in a certain year, and further in a given month in that year, he would reach the summit of whatever his profession was, and that he would at that moment hold the highest position that his career could confer on him.

He carefully took a note of what I told him, and then in a rather mocking way he said : "And now, sir, as you have gone so far you may as well make a guess at the exact day of this wonderful event."

"Call it a guess if you wish," I replied, "but by my calculations the day should be any one of those days which make by addition -the figure of I in the month of July 1894, such as the 1st, 10th, 19th or 28th."

This he carefully noted, and then when I asked him to give me an impression of his hand for my collection he turned and said : "You shall have it on one of the days you have mentioned, provided your predictions should become verified," and so my strange visitor left.

Some three years passed, and I had completely forgotten the incident, when one morning a messenger called and without any explanation informed me that my attendance was required at twelve o'clock that day at the High Courts of Justice.

I will not enter into my feelings or tell you my fears, but in a very nervous state of mind I went with the man and finally found myself waiting in a badly furnished room at the back of one of the principal Courts.

Minute after minute passed until nearly an hour had gone. I had imagined myself tried and executed in a hundred different ways, when suddenly a side door opened and the Lord Chief Justice appeared before me in all the majesty of his robes of office.

I admit I did not recognise my client of some years before, but, without waiting a moment, rolling up his ermine sleeves, he said: " I am willing to keep my promise; you can have impression of my hands now."

I had no apparatus for doing such work with me, but there was not a moment to be lost. I lit a legal looking candle standing on the table, blackened some sheets of paper which the Lord Chief Justice himself found in a drawer, and in a few minutes I had obtained an excellent impression of his hands.

Taking a pen he wrote "Russell of Killowen," with the date, and simply said : "You see I have kept my promise; this is the first day I have put on these robes as Lord Chief Justice of England-your date was exact, though how you did it I cannot imagine."

As it may interest my readers the impression is here reproduced, and the curious thing is that the imprint of the High Courts of Justice which was on the paper he gave me can also be clearly seen in the impression at the ball of the thumb.

CHAPTER XXIX

THE TWO CHAMBERLAINS : HEREDITY : THE RIGHT HAND A. J. BALFOUR AND OTHER DISTINGUISHED PERSONS

A NOTHER interesting interview which I had about this time was with Mr. Joseph Chamberlain and also one with his son Mr. Austen Chamberlain.

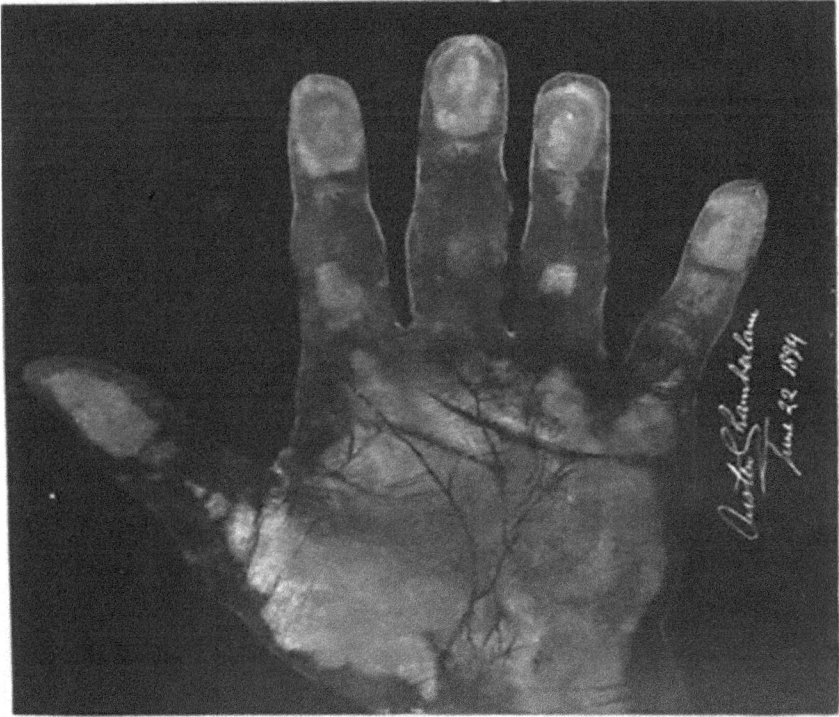

THE RIGHT HON. AUSTEN CHAMBERLAIN, M.P.
Example of Heredity— see plate showing the lines on Mr. Joseph Chamberlain's hand

On the morning of June 23, 1894, I had called at the House of Commons to keep an appointment made for me with Mr. Joseph Chamberlain.

My theory of heredity as shown by the lines of the hands appeared to interest him deeply. I showed him an impression which I had just taken off the right hand of his' son Mr. Austen Chamberlain, and together we compared the "markings" with those on his own hand.

117

The two impressions which I reproduce in this book will bear out what I have said previously about heredity.

I would like especially to draw the attention of my readers to the centre line going from the wrist towards the second finger and at the end turning towards the first finger. This line is called the, line of Individuality or mark of Destiny, and when turning towards the first finger it indicates that the Individuality will point, lead or dictate to others-the first finger is also called the Law giver or Dictator, and with the strong line running upward from the Line of Life under the first finger seems strangely appropriate to the career of Mr. Joseph Chamberlain, and also to the future which is indicated for the son who has followed in the political career of his distinguished father.

Another distinguished Member of Parliament who gave me an impression of his hand was Mr. Balfour. This was signed, as will be seen by the following plate, A. J. B. 7/6/95.

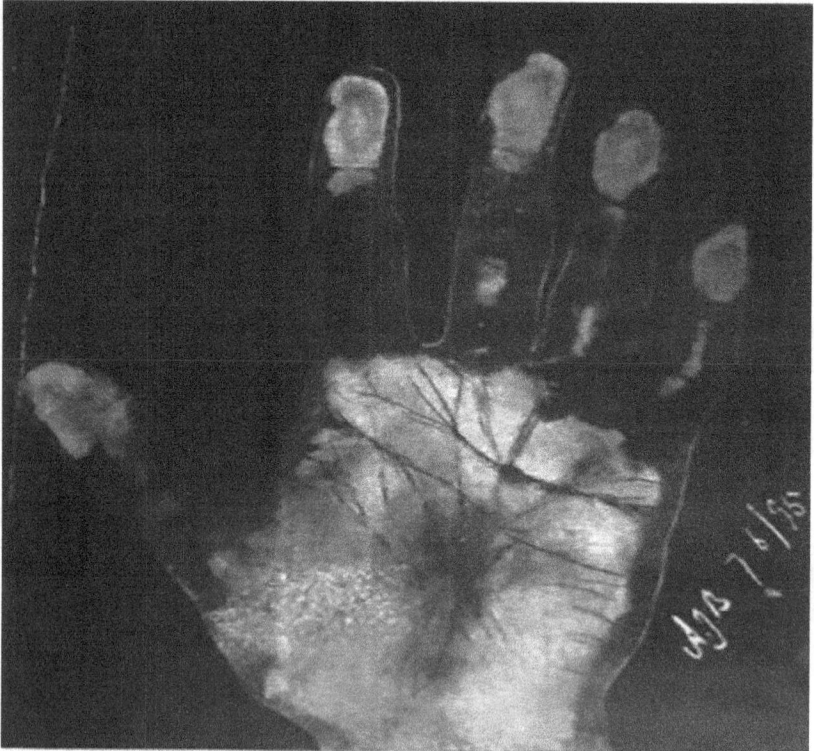

THE RIGHT HON. A. J. BALFOUR. M.P.

The important lines to the first finger will in this case also be noticed, but the most casual observer will remark that the whole character of

Example of Heredity-see plate showing the lines on Mr. Joseph Chamberlain's hand this type is distinctly different from that represented in the impressions of the hands of the two Chamberlains. It denotes more the type of the philosopher than that of the dictator; it is too sensitive a type ever to take full advantage of the opportunities that would cross its path, but it will be noticed that the horizontal line (the line of Mentality) is so long and well marked that it traverses the whole palm.

In such a book as this it would be out of place and wearisome to my readers if I asked them to follow me through a more detailed description of the markings of character in the impressions of the hands which I subjoin here, but for those who have knowledge of the subject the appended reproductions will speak for themselves.

OTHER INTERVIEWS WITH DISTINGUISHED PERSONS

I will not in this volume dwell longer on the many interviews I had with distinguished personalities on the occasion of my second visit to London. Suffice it to say that among the many others who consulted me or gave me auto graphed impressions of their hands were the Duchess of Leinster, the Countess of Aberdeen, S.A.R. le Comte de Paris, S.A.R. the Infanta_ Eulalie, Lord Kitchener of Khartoum (at that time General Kitchener), Lord Charles Beresford, the Duke of Newcastle, the Rev. J. Page Hopps, Robert Hichens, Lieut.-Col. Ponsonby, Sir Henry Drummond Wolff, the Rev. Godfrey Biddulph, Madame Sarah Grand, John Strange Winter, Mrs. Florence Fenwick Miller, Mrs. Annie Besant, Sir Edwin Arnold, Sir John Lubbock, Lord Leighton (President of the Royal Academy), Sir Arthur Sullivan, Lady Paget, Lady Henry Somerset, Madame Melba, Madame Calve, General Sir Redvers Buller, &c. &c.

For fear of tiring my readers I will not carry these Memoirs farther for the present than the end of my second visit to London.

It will I think be sufficient here to say that I travelled and lectured on the subject all over the States.

I was invited to speak sometimes in churches, as for example, at the People's Church in St, Paul, in Boston, Chicago and other cities, and on other occasions before the great Methodist organisation, the Chautauqua; at some of these places my audience often numbered between two and three thousand persons, and the greatest interest in the subject was aroused by these lectures.

In my next book I shall deal principally with my experiences in America, giving full particulars of interviews with the then President, Mr. Grover Cleveland, and Mrs. Cleveland, together with the principal members of his Government. I shall also tell of some curious episodes with clients in America, and also of my life in Paris, where I had many varied experiences and where I met some remarkable personalities, such as King Leopold of Belgium, The Shah of Persia, Prince Louis Napoleon, Prince Karageorgevitch of Servia, the great astronomer Camille Flammarion, the famous Doctor Evans (Marquis d'Oyley), Archbishop Ireland, Monseigneur O'Connell of Rome, and the principal members of the English and American Colonies.

I will speak of these persons and tell of them, not perhaps as the world imagines them, but simply as in the light of my own experience I found them to be.

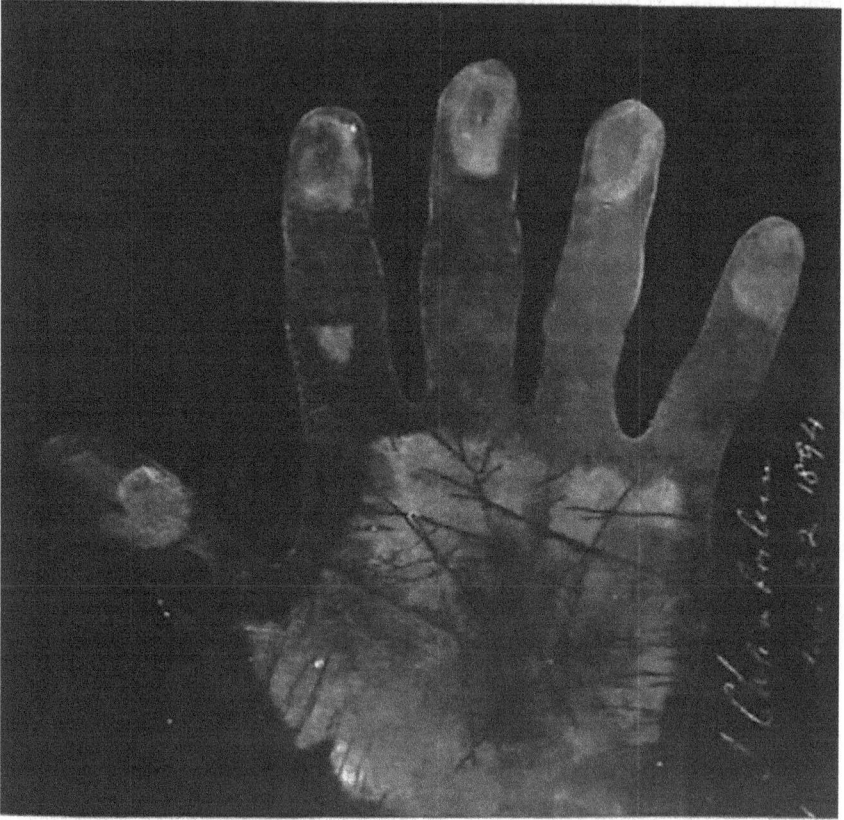

THE RIGHT HON. JOSEPH CHAMBERLAIN, M.P.
Example of Heredity—see the lines on Mr. Austen Chamberlain's
hand in the following illustration

CHAPTER XXX

CONCLUSION

IN conclusion, in giving this first book of Memoirs to the public, I trust I shall not be accused of having attempted to do anything but give a simple and straightforward account of a strange career and nothing more.

But to believers or sceptics one word I must add, and that is, that though we may never be able to penetrate the mystery of " how such things can be," yet this is no reason for saying that they do not exist. As it is impossible to solve the mystery of life itself, so is it not possible to follow the meaning of all its manifestations.

Every day some new truth is being stumbled across by investigators of all classes, but in the investigation of that which concerns the soul side of life the mystery may be all the greater but none the less true for that.

Life, purpose, and design are so intimately woven together by the loom of Destiny that our earthly eyes may well be satisfied if they but see the pattern and no more.

One thing is certain-the occult side of life is the real life that like a thread of gold binds all together. It is the soul life of things that are and that will be. It finds its expression in shapes and forms and lines, writes its history in people, uses nations as the servants of its pur pose, and, from the veriest atom to the greatest, none can escape the destiny of being part of the purpose of life, whatever that purpose may be.

But it is as a great power for good that I would make an appeal on behalf of occultism. It is for this reason that, like a missionary who has found the truth, I would fain see every member of life's community interested in it in some form or another.

As it is the heart of all religion, so is it in its turn the greatest religion of all.

It is the one in whose temple all religions may meet, where Catholic and Protestant, Mahometan or Hebrew may find something in common, from which they may trace the origin of their own ceremonial and know the reason why such ceremonial was made by those whose footsteps have long since been lost in the dust of centuries. The Hebrew would find in it why the number twelve was selected as the number of his tribes, and the Christian would see the same truth in the number of the Apostles.

The Temple of Solomon would no longer be a dumb pile of marvellous masonry, but a revelation of God's command to Moses on the Mount, "Be sure that thou makest it according to the pattern which I showed thee in the Heavens," (namely, in accordance with the scheme of creation itself, as manifested in the Twelve signs of the Zodiac which in the Temple represented the Twelve Tribes of Israel, these again being prophetic of the twelve apostles of Christ).

To the Christian the ceremonial of his religion would be explained, and even the consecration service of a Catholic Cathedral would assume an occult importance little guessed at, perhaps, by even the priests who carry out the ceremony; thus we have the twelve crosses emblematic of the twelve houses of the Zodiac; the seven candles representing the seven creative planets that control the Grand Man of the Universe, seven being also the spiritual number in all creation; the four crosses drawn on the four corners of the High Altar, symbolic of the four corner-stones of the year, the four signs of the seasons and so on.

The oft-repeated prayer, "Thy Will be done on earth as it is in Heaven" (or in the Heavens), would have a fuller meaning if translated by the light of occultism.

The thirty-three years' ministry of Christ, corresponding as it did to a Solar cycle, with his crucifixion at a certain hour and on a certain "day of the week," would no longer appear to be accidental or mysterious if read by the only key which can and does unravel such things.

Under these conditions religion itself would become a living force, and not the intangible maze of ceremonials that it is to-day.

Men and women would no longer be the puppets of paid priests, but their every action would become an act of prayer, a daily service of adoration to the Creator who has created all in His infinite wisdom.

No more broken suicides and wasted lives would line life's pathway as they do to-day, for all would know their purpose, the duties they are best fitted for, and when and how to act, so that they might achieve success, happiness, and the greater fulfilment of their destiny.

Believe me, it was never the purpose of the Creator that men and women should be the unhappy beasts of burden that they are to-day, instead of the contented co-workers of His infinite purpose, but as time is nothing in the eyes of the Eternal, so does it take centuries for man to learn the story of his creation-the story that is written in all things-and the last story which he ever reads.

The struggle from the beginning has been between the two forces, non-belief and faith the two forces alluded to in all sacred books, always struggling for the mastery.

But faith is the first-born of God, the heir that neither time nor tears can dispossess, and so in the end will occult knowledge possess the earth-and "the crooked ways shall be made straight."

The usefulness of occultism lies in its strength to withstand the trials of daily life, its faith in the unfolding of the purpose —-its patience to wait the appointed time.

The true occultist failure does not break, nor success blind with its glory, and if one or the other comes, ·he but learns the lesson and is thankful.

Such are a few reasons that prompt me to send these Memoirs on their way. They may interest those already interested in such matters, and those who are not they may perhaps lead to examine such questions for themselves, and so swell the steadily increasing band of men and women who stem the tide of Materialism and prevent humanity from forgetting that "the mystery of the world is the visible not the invisible."

FINIS

Cheiro's Book of Numbers

Chaldean Numerology Explained

Cheiro

Hardcover 978-1-940849-30-0
Paperback 978-1-957990-01-9
eBook   978-1-940849-29-4

Sample from Cheiro's Book of Numbers

IT naturally follows that if a person should make a special study of any one subject, from long experience, cultivation and studious research, he will in the end unravel, at least to some extent, the so-called mysteries of the subject on which he has so concentrated his attention.

To the student of Art, Art reveals her mysteries of colour, form, design, pose, and a thousand and one subtleties that escape the ordinary observer. To the student of Biology every leaf tells its own story, every tree its age, every flower its own pedigree.

To the student of Science, what is magic to the uninitiated becomes a natural phenomenon with general laws, governed by rules or calculations that all who choose can learn and understand.

In presenting this book to the public I need then offer no other apology for so doing, than that of having been a student of this particular branch of thought for a very long period, and having proved so-called theories by countless experiments and experiences, I feel I am at last in a position to give to the world at large the result of such studies.

It is admitted by all that the occult side of things has been the one side of life the least explored or investigated.

That there is an occult or hidden part in actual relation to human life is on every side a conceded fact, but before this mystery-the greatest of all-the majority of thinkers have held themselves aloof.

In our age the physical and mechanical sciences have called for the greatest attention, yet such things as wireless communication and radium, to-day household words, have been stumbled across by so-called chance.

Already wireless communication has saved hundreds of lives, radium has done likewise, the mysteries of yesterday have become the commonplaces of to-day, and so knowledge in the eternal fitness of things becomes the servant of those who serve.

In pursuit of the laws which have controlled thought in recent centuries, man has, in earning his successes on the physical and mechanical plane, forgotten the loss he has sustained from the lack of study and observation on the occult or psychic side of humanity. He is more occupied to-day in building implements for the destruction of life than he is in the problems of life itself, or in the finding out of those laws which create, control, and sustain life.

When Newton discovered gravitation, it was not supposed for a moment that he had solved the problem of the spheres, and it is sometimes forgotten that when he came to realise that beyond our system of stars, sun, moon and planets there were again the "fixed stars" with their countless systems, in the magnitude of the problem, he could only decide that there was again some occult law behind all, greater than any known law that could even be imagined.

With these few words as a preface, I will endeavour to make my theory so clear that I hope anyone of ordinary intelligence may be able to follow and experiment with certain rules which will be treated in the following chapters.

During my earlier years, when travelling in the East, it had been my good fortune to come in contact with a certain sect of Brahmins who had kept in their hands from almost prehistoric times studies and practices of an occult nature which they regarded as sacredly as they did their own religious teachings. Among other things, they permitted me to learn certain theories on the occult significance of numbers and their influence and relation to human life, which subsequent years and manifold experiences not only confirmed, but justified me in endeavouring to apply them in a practical sense so that others might also use this knowledge with, I hope, advantage to themselves and to those around them.

The ancient Hindu searchers after Nature's laws, it must be remembered, were in former years masters of all such studies, but in transmitting their knowledge to their descendants, they so endeavoured to hide their secrets from the common people that in most cases the key to the problem became lost, and the truth that had been discovered became buried in the dust of superstition and chariatanism, to be re-formed, let us hope, when some similar cycle of thought in its own appointed time will again claim attention to this side of nature.

This ancient people, together with the Chaldeans and Egyptians, were the absolute masters of the occult or hidden meaning of numbers, in their application to time and in their relation to human life. When examining such questions, we must not forget that it was the Hindus who discovered what is known as the precession of the Equinoxes, and in their calculation such an occurrence takes place every 25,827 years; our modern science after labours of hundreds of years has simply proved them to be correct.

How, or by what means they were able to arrive at such a calculation, has never been discovered-observations lasting over such a period of time are hardly admissible, and calculation without instruments is also scarcely conceivable, and so science has only been able, first to accept their statement, and later to acknowledge its accuracy. Their judgment, together with that of the Chaldeans, as to the length of what is now known as the cycle of years of the planets, has been handed down to us from the most remote ages, and also by our modern appliances has been proved correct, so when one comes to a study such as this, as to the value of the numbers 1 to 9, which, as the seven harmonies of music are the bases of all music that has ever been conceived, these above-stated numbers are the basis of all our numbers and calculations, it is then only logical to accept the decisions of those great students of long past ages and at least examine their deductions with a mind free from bias and prejudice.

It is impossible in a book of this size to give in detail all the reasonings and examples that exist for a belief in the occult side of numbers, but it may interest my readers if I give a few illustrations of why the number 7 has for ages been regarded as the number of mystery relating to the spiritual side of things, and why the number 9 has in its turn come to be regarded as the finality or end of the series on which all our materialistic calculations are built, but the most casual observer can only admit that beyond the number 9 all ordinary numbers become but a mere repetition of the first 9. A simple illustration of this will readily suffice. The number 10, as the zero is not a number, becomes a repetition of the number 1. The number n added together as the ancient occultists laid down in their law of natural addition namely, adding together from left to right, repeats the number 2, 12 repeats 3, 13 repeats 4, and so on up to 19, which in its turn becomes i plus 9 equals 10, and so again the repetition of 1. 20 represents 2, and so on to infinity.

The occult symbolism of what are called compound numbers that is, those numbers from 10 onwards, I will explain later. In this way it will be seen that in all our materialistic systems of numbers, the numbers 1 to 9 are the base on which we are compelled to build, just as in the same way the seven great or primary harmonies in music are the bases of all music, and again as the seven primary colours are the bases of all our combinations of colours. In passing it may be remarked that all through the Bible and other sacred books, the "seven," whenever mentioned, always stands in relation to the spiritual or mysterious God force, and has a curious significance in this sense whenever employed. For a few instances of this, take the seven days (or cycles) of the creation as referred to in Genesis:

The seven heavens, so often referred to.
The seven thrones.
The seven seals.
The seven churches.

The seven days' march round the walls of Jericho, when on "the seventh day," the walls fell. before that mysterious to the magnetic influences of the seven creative planets which radiate through the earth.

Again, we have the seven Spirits referred to in theEgyptian religion.
The seven Devas of the Hindus' Bible.
The seven Amschaspands of Persian faith.
The seven Angels of the Chaldeans.
The seven Sephiroth of the Hebrew Cabala.
The seven Archangels of Revelation, etc. etc.

Let us now take another view of this strange number.

If we were to examine every class of occult teaching from the Hindu, Chinese, Egyptian, Greek, Hebrew, or modern school, whichever one may choose, in every case-and without a single exception-we shall find that the quality of the number 7 stands for the expression of that mysterious God force in Nature before referred to.

In the most ancient rules of occult philosophy we find the rule laid down that the number 7 is the only number capable of dividing "the number of Eternity," and continuing in itself as long as the number representing Eternity lasts, and yet, at every addition of itself producing the number 9, or in other words it produces the basic number on which all materialistic calculations are built and on which all human beings depend and the whole edifice of human thought finds expression.

EXAMPLE

The number i is the first number. It represents the First Cause, Creator, God or Spirit, call it as you like. A circle or the zero, "0," has always been taken as the symbol of endlessness-otherwise Eternity. Place the 1 and the figure zero by its side, and you get the significant symbol of eternity such as 1 plus 0, the 10, and then, place as many of these emblems of eternity side by side as you like, and you get such a figure as 1,000,000. Divide by the mystic number 7 and you get the number 142857.

7)1,000,000
142857.

Add as many zeros as you like, and keep on dividing by the 7, and you yourself may go on through all eternity and you can only get repetitions of the same 142857, which from tune immemorial has been called the "sacred number."

Now add this number wherever you find it by natural addition, it will give you the figure 27, and as you have seen by the rule of natural addition described on a preceding page, you keep adding till only one number remains, to arrive at what is known as "the root of the number." You add again 27 by natural addition, and 2 plus 7 equals 9, or in other words, you get the full range of the first series of numbers on which all materialistic or human calculations can be built.

Now, let us return to the symbolism of seven for a moment. You know. of course, that Buddha is always represented as sitting in the centre of a Lotus. Let us examine, then, the secret of such a selection. It is not perhaps generally known that the 7 is reproduced in many strange ways in Nature herself, and that flowers that have not been crossed by intermingling with other flowers have their outside petals in the number of seven, but as flowers are so easily crossed with other varieties, and it is so difficult to find a pure type, Buddha took the Lotus, which never becomes crossed or loses its individuality, as the emblem of the religion he taught, because, first, its seven foundation petals are always in evidence, and further, the religion he taught was that the creative Spirit was the foundation and origin 'f all things, and thus again bore silent but unmistakable testimony to the creative action of the seven planetsfrom which all religions have had their origin.

Long before man made his creeds, or civilisations their laws, the influence of these seven planets had become known on the earth. Out of the dark night of antiquity their light became law, and as far as we can penetrate, even to the very confines of prehistoric days, in all races, in all countries, we find the influence of the seven planets through all and in all.

The seven days of the week have been the outcome of the influence of the seven creative planets and gave the names of the days of the week, in every land or clime.

Take any nation you may choose, this fact remains the same, and is so expressed in almost every language, Chinese, Assyrian, Hindu, Egyptian, Hebrew, Greek, Latin, French, German, or English. In modern languages Monday or Moonsday in English becomes Montag in German or Lundi Lune) in French, Lunes in Spanish, and so on until one comes to Saturday or Saturn's day, the day on which God ordered the Hebrews that no work should be done, and in giving them this command He said, "It is a sign between Me and the children of Israel for ever." And, strange as it may seem, Saturday, year by year, in our modern civilization is becoming more and ore a day of rest.

In connection with this thought, it is worthy of remark that Saturn, the last planet in the series of the seven creative planets of our solar system, in all religions, Hebrew or otherwise, represents "cessation," or rest from labour in another sense. In this strange example one can see the connection between the seven days of the week and the seven creative planets, and it throws a new light on the verse, "God made the sun, moon and stars and appointed them for signs and for seasons and for days and for years." Even Mr. Maunder, the eminent author of so many works on astronomy, calls attention to this strange division of the week into seven days when he says in his Astronomy of the Bible: "the period of seven days does not fit precisely into either months or seasons of the year. It is not a division of time that man would naturally adopt, it runs across all natural division of time," but this author, not seeing or perhaps knowing the great hidden truth contained in the number 7, worried only over the point, that it was not "a division of time which man would naturally adopt."

But as everything on the earth and above the earth has its meaning, and especially its secret or soul meaning, its place, position, and number, in the "order of things," which is the highest form of design, every day of the week, every hour of the day, and every minute of the hour, has both its meaning and number.

It is invariably conceded by every class of scientist that the regularity, order, and system of the wonderful machinery of the heavens is beyond all comparison. We know to-day that the heavenly bodies move through their orbits with such precision that in millions of years they do not vary one minute of time. We know that they exercise an influence on this earth which is felt by the veriest atoms in the earth, though what this force is, or with what incredible speed it acts, may forever remain a mystery. It was in dealing with this mysterious law that the ancient philosophers by study, experiments, concentration of mind, and perhaps intuition, arrived at the fixation of certain laws governing life, which may be as accurate as their discovery that the "precession of the Equinoxes takes place once in every 25,827 years."

It is from these wonderful students of Nature that we have received the first idea as to the divisions of the Zodiac into twelve periods of 30 degrees, and further, that each period produces a definite and well-known influence on the earth and on human beings born in any of its twelve periods.

They further subdivided these 30-degree periods into divisions of three periods of 10 degrees -each, in which the planets are also found to have an influence, and they pursued then- investigations until they worked out a system demonstrating that each day had its own particular meaning due to vibrations in the ether, which keeps the earth in instantaneous report with its entire solar system, and lastly that as the sun enters a new degree of the Zodiac in mid-winter at about the rate of every 21/2 to 3 minutes, and in summer at the rate of 3 to 4 3/4 minutes, that its magnetic influence varied the effect of the vibrations or ether waves of each planet, and so enabled these students of Nature to carry their system in this way down to almost the smallest fraction of time. [5]

In examining this subject, let us take for an example any remarkable piece of mechanism we may have seen such as a clock. We have noticed how wheel fits into wheel and how the entire mechanism is put into motion as the ray or tooth of the governing wheel presses against the tooth of the next, and so on.

Keeping this illustration in your mind for a moment, let us regard the 360 degrees of the Zodiac into which the sun appears to pass, from degree to degree on an average of every 4 minutes as the teeth of one of our wheels. This 360 degrees multiplied by the 4 minutes gives 1,440

5   This applies of course, to the motion of the sun through the symbolic or cabbalistic Zodiac used in the East.

minutes, and this, divided by 60, to bring it to hours, gives us the 24-hour day, which becomes in its turn another spoke in the great wheel of time, and onsequently, by the advance of the sun, must bring us to the commencement of another day under new and distinct influences, and so on until the year itself is completed.

THE TWELVE SIGNS OF THE ZODIAC[6]

I. Aries, the Ram
II. Taurus, the Bull
III. Gemini, the Twins
IV. Cancer, the Crab
V. Leo, the Lion
VI. Virgo, the Virgin
VII. Libra, the Balance
VIII. Scorpio, the Scorpion
IX. Sagittarius, the Archer
X. Capricorn, the Goat
XI. Aquarius, the Water-Bearer
XII. Pisces, the Fishes

This map represents the Sun's entry into Aries in the Vernal equinox on March 21-23 of every year. The letters at the points of the central cross stand for: OR-Oriental or Eastern; MC-Mid-Heaven; OC-Occidental or Western; FC-Lower Heaven.

Now as science proves that it takes the sun 30 days to pass from one division of the Zodiac into another, again we have the illustration of another wheel, as it were, but a still slower one, being put into motion, and consequently with the change in the heavenly mechanism another set of influences are brought to bear upon the earth, and so on until the twelve months of the year have in their turn experienced the influence of the sun in the twelve divisions of the Zodiac.

Let us now return for a moment to the part played by the seven creative planets. No one to-day, I believe, can plead ignorance of the effect of one of these planets, namely the moon, on the earth itself and on the people who inhabit the earth. We all know, or at least have heard, about the effect of the moon on the brain of people mentally unbalanced. We know how it causes tides to rise and fall. along our shores, but still perhaps we do not realise that even in the deepest ocean its pull or attraction is

---

6   Use these symbols with the illustration on the next page.

so great that it causes hundreds of thousands of tons of dead weight of water to be drawn up by it to such a height as 70 feet in the Bay of Fundy and in the Bristol Channel.

Scientists, like Darwin in England, Flammarion in France, and others in Germany, made the startling discovery that there are actually tides in the solid earth itself, which are affected by the attraction of the moon. What then of the effect of the moon on the brain itself, which contains the most subtle essence and is one of the greatest mysteries known in life? Granted that this be admitted, what then of the part played on human nature by the rest of the planets, which are in each individual case far larger than the moon? The following table showing the dimensions of each of the planets will illustrate better than any words I may use this side of the argument.

Diameter of Mercury	*2,000 miles.*
the Moon	*2,100 miles.*
Venus	*7.510 miles.*
the Earth	*7913 miles.*
Mars	*4,920 miles.*
Jupiter	*88,390 miles.*
Saturn	*71,900 miles.*
Uranus	*33,000 miles.*
Neptune	*36,000 miles.*
the Sun	*860,000 miles.*

I ask, is it logical, with such a demonstration before one, to admit the effect of the moon and to deny any effect to the other planets that are in fact so much larger than it?

Let us now return to the important side of the question as regards the rules set forth in this book. You will very naturally ask, how and when were such numbers arrived at that represent the mechanical action or influence of the celestial system on the people of this earth? I could write an entire volume on this side of the question alone, but in the following necessarily condensed pages you will find the general law explained which may be sufficient to elucidate the system contained in the following chapters.

www.ingramcontent.com/pod-product-compliance
Lightning Source LLC
Chambersburg PA
CBHW070834100426
42813CB00003B/616